D1086918

Turning Oil Green

A Market-Based Path to Renewables

Dan Dicker

ISBN 978-0-9964897-6-8

Contents

Preface

This book, I suppose, is the sum of my 35-year career in oil. I started off as a trader in the pits of the New York Mercantile Exchange, and although I was curious when I first started trading in my 20s about how the global energy markets worked, that curiosity in those days didn't compel me much. I was more interested in making a living and trying to figure out which direction oil futures prices might go that day – or more important to me, that minute. But as the years rolled along, and I was exposed to more parts of the global energy chain through their necessary engagement with the fast-growing power of the futures markets, it became useful and often profitable to understand the agendas of the bigger players I was already indirectly in contact with – the large and growing investment banks like Morgan Stanley and Goldman Sachs; the smaller, new independent oil companies concentrating on the fracking of natural gas and then oil, including companies like Chesapeake, EOG, and Continental; the bigger multi-national mega-cap energy majors (Exxon and Chevron, etc.); and even the oil-producing sovereign nations of the Middle East inside OPEC, most notably Saudi Arabia and Iraq.

A media opportunity that began when the first Gulf War was just about to live its short life in the early 1990s grew into a returning presence on CNBC and other financial networks, and a columnist's position at TheStreet.com, where speaking and writing intelligently about the movements of the oil markets and the underlying stocks attached to them required much more knowledge and understanding of the many inputs into the energy markets and their influences. The last 20 years added to my previous 15 and as I continued to trade, I developed a more macro understanding of how and why the energy markets operated as they did. I wrote two books in 2011 and 2015 about how the oil markets worked, with the hope of making folks more aware of the important but less understood inputs that moved the price of this most important commodity, and also to give some insight on where some better investments in the energy sector might likely be found.

This book has a very different purpose in mind.

I believe my liberal political leanings are somewhat rare among experts in the energy area, and therefore I had some unique insights that most others did not see, or were less able to tell. Most energy folks I've met are conservative and view the Left as anti-business and devoutly opposed to any and all fossil fuels. Similarly, I have met few in the 'Green' community who view the motivations in the energy world beyond a blanket belief that everyone in it is evil and on the hunt for profits, with little regard for anything else. I, on the other hand, think that I have come to appreciate the truths—and the hyperbolic falsehoods—of both sides.

As I have witnessed the timeline on climate change shorten and become more dire, I've felt a need to use my perspective to put these two groups together, and advance a practical plan that both energy folks and environmentalists might be able to agree on. I hit upon the simple idea of viewing the energy world as an evolving system with stages towards 'perfection,' as we might view man's evolution progressing towards our present modern form. But I also saw that the energy world had been stalled in its progress towards the next logical stage—sustainable and renewable energy—particularly since the oil crash of 2014, and I set out to understand why and how those roadblocks could be removed and that natural evolution resumed and even accelerated.

The ascent of Donald Trump as President stopped my lei-surely reflections and forced me to start deeper research and begin writing this book. I had been seeing far too slow, but at least steady, progress towards renewables before the Trump administration came to power. The Paris Accords were a guideline towards reduced carbon emissions; electric cars were gaining wider acceptance courtesy of Tesla; coal plants were disappearing steadily; and even oil company sharehold-ers were demanding, and getting, a better and more responsi-ble approach towards climate change.

But the actions of the Trump administration have worked to stop all that progress and even turn back the clock where it could on our energy evolution – by at least 30 years. Besides walking away from the Paris Accords, they began removing many regulatory guidelines involving oil and gas production as fast as they could, began opening up drilling on all Federal lands, chopping CAFE guidelines for motor vehicles and a dozen more initiatives, even advocating a resurgence of coal through incentives from the Energy department and FERC – a terrific idea if the year were 1920, not 2020. I reached my own breaking point the day after this tweet came out in 2018, and I began working on this book:

Donald J. Trump ●
@realDonaldTrump

Follow ∨

California wildfires are being magnified & made so much worse by the bad environmental laws which aren't allowing massive amounts of readily available water to be properly utilized. It is being diverted into the Pacific Ocean. Must also tree clear to stop fire from spreading!

4:53 PM - 6 Aug 2018

This tweet was the President's reaction to the vastly destruc-tive wildfires that had been raging in California during the summer of 2018, an historic year that included many other extreme climate anomalies including hurricanes, acute heat, and droughts around the world. I considered just laughing, and ignoring this tweet – after all, that reaction had worked before.

In fact, I've often viewed the energy world as much as a comedy as I have a drama. Here's a short energy story unrelated to our current purpose that will demonstrate: I can remember the scramble to build liquid natural gas (LNG) import facilities in the early 2000s as natural gas traded regularly and expensively above $10. The idea was to bring cheaper natural gas in from abroad, using an expensive process of cooling natural gas and transporting it in a liquid form in very specialized refrigerated tankers. Billions of dollars and normally 5-10 years are needed to get these LNG import and regasification projects to completion, first waiting for Federal approval to build, gathering the capital guarantees, and then doing the long construction work that each one of these massive projects requires.

Most of this money and time were ultimately wasted, however, as production of domestic natural gas from fracking during the 2000s exceeded everyone's expectations and flooded the domestic markets, crashing prices at precisely the same time these LNG import projects were just beginning to come online. Of course, the cheaper prices of domestic surplus fracked gas made importing LNG from afar ridiculous, and billions of dollars were lost.

But the story doesn't end there. As the domestic natural gas glut has become a fixture of U.S. markets since, many 'smart' energy companies have tried to recoup some of their losses in these same projects by converting those same import facilities to export facilities. Conversion from one to the other is also very expensive and time-intensive, but much of the underlying infrastructure is the same for either import or export use and was already standing there, so it seemed like a reasonable idea for new LNG import terminals that were otherwise just sitting around growing weeds. Many more billions were thrown in during the 2010s, trying to take advantage of the now-low prices of domestic natural gas, and the relatively high prices in other countries.

Figure P.1.
Daily Natural Gas Deliveries for LNG Fall off a Cliff

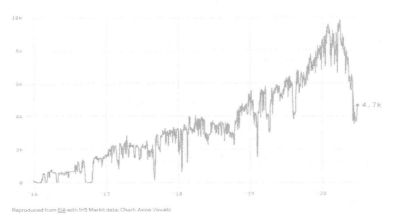

Reproduced from EIA with IHS Markit data; Chart: Axios Visuals

But since 2018 and particularly in 2020 because of the coronavirus, we've seen the market for LNG export collapse worldwide, as seen in Figure P.1, as surplus gas supplies appear everywhere and prices around the globe for natural gas make historic new lows. In addition, other major exporters of LNG in Qatar and Australia are competing more successfully with newly built LNG exporters here in the U.S.

Again, with superb timing, many of those newly repurposed export facilities that undertook the conversion from import to export plants in the early teens and are just now coming online are scrambling, mostly unsuccessfully, to find even marginally profitable export contracts. Those few who have already been converted and are ready to finally work again are more likely to now sit idly, as they did as import terminals before. Freeport, Dominion, Kinder Morgan, and Sempra are four energy companies that are having a whole lot more trouble than they planned making the multi-billion-dollar investments in those facilities pay for themselves. Other export projects nearing completion from Exxon, Shell, and Energy Transfer have been suddenly abandoned or sold with their own large, stranded losses.

Call me a bit strange, but I really find this stuff hilarious. Get the boom wrong, then compound the mistake by getting the bust wrong as well. It's particularly funny because this boom/bust type of grossly mismanaged cycling of prices from energy companies is hardly restricted to wasted investments in LNG. Over my 35 years of observation, I've witnessed this recurring theme in the "oil patch," both from individual companies and the industry as a whole, so many times, I can hardly count. (In fact, much of this book is committed to outlining just this kind of capital black hole that's been the story for fracking here in the United States.)

To add a possible second punchline, the future missteps for LNG here in the U.S. might not stop even with this latest round of waste. Will a radical Democratic administration come to power and make all oil and gas fracking grossly restrictive, or even illegal? That exact plank was in the platforms of at least two Democratic nominees for President in the last primaries (Bernie Sanders and Elizabeth Warren), so it's hardly impossible. Draconian Federal restrictions on fracking would surely send prices for natural gas soaring again like in the early aughts, and might convince these terminal owners to invest once again to revert their newly christened export terminals back to their original importing function. Knowing the energy world as I do, and their ability to take a two-time loser and make it three, I wouldn't doubt it.

But back to Trump. I wasn't laughing much when I saw that tweet from late 2018 from the President of the United States. It truly hit me like a ton of bricks, and it demanded I get to work. Every word of it is ignorant and dangerous, minimizing the severity and frequency of California's two major resource challenges of water and wildfires, blaming environmentalists for both problems, and denying global warming and its effects to boot.

More distressingly to me, this tweet – and the entirety of carbon burning and climate change as a national and global issue – has since shrunk into the background as hundreds of other outrageous tweets and actions of this President have continued to mount. This, to me, is the biggest travesty of all. I have seen negligible focus from the major networks and newspapers on climate change since Trump was inaugurated, as they choose to cover other political and cultural conflicts that this President has caused. I don't minimize any of the other damage that Trump has inflicted to this country in his tenure, but I find all of these outrages to be superficial compared to the time bomb of global warming. There is the hope that whatever else Trump has done to destroy norms, alliances, and institutions, all of it can be put right again, given the right leaders and the right intentions of the public.

But climate change and global warming are on a disaster timeline – a timeline that cannot be reversed. Every day that is lost without making positive strides to control carbon output is a day that can't be retrieved, and makes the battles to avoid reaching critical temperature thresholds that much more difficult to win. I felt I had to push whatever focus I could back on this most imperative issue, and moreover inspire an honest and practical discussion on what can be done to really move – right now and in our divided country – the natural progression of energy sources towards renewables.

I'm not sure anyone will completely like what I have to say. I don't spare anyone some blame for the mess we're currently in. Even though I have an obvious liberal bent, I don't hold the left wing and environmental lobbies faultless in trying to create a truly practical climate change plan. In all cases, while their intentions are good, they are often poorly informed about the mechanisms of the markets and the many positives that come from energy exploration and production—with our national security, tens of thousands of well-paying jobs within the industry, and the many other related industries that rely on domestic oil and gas.

I like to ask extremely radical left wingers when I meet them if they like their iPhones and whether they'd like to see whether they would operate well without fossil fuels to provide both the raw materials and power to manufacture them and then use them. It's a vicious question, I'll admit, but it tries to make the point that oil and gas are a necessary part of our modern world, will likely be a significant part forever, and we couldn't do much at all without them.

Most Green initiatives I have seen that look to starve fossil fuel companies—such as the divestiture movement of college endowments, or "green funds," or the attempt to completely remove Federal oil and gas subsidies, or the lawsuits that immediately get filed against any new oil or gas pipeline, or the Northeast anti-fracking campaigns, or many of the pieces of the Green New Deal—all of these, instead of furthering the cause, have, in my view, helped slow down the "natural evolution" of energy instead, not speed it up. The blanket hate of all fossil fuels from the Left has worked to try to cordon energy companies away from the renewable revolution, almost as a punishment, when those same companies are by far the best equipped to get us there the quickest. They know more about how energy is harnessed, transported, converted, and utilized than anyone else by far and need to be an integral part of our solution, if we are to finally have one that works.

The analogy I often use is the U.S. invasion of Iraq, where the Baathist ruling class was thrown out from their roles in government and Iraq's underlying infrastructure management by Paul Bremer, leading the American ruling force in 2003. Unfortunately, those Iraqis were the only ones who knew where all the levers were and how they worked. So, when the power plants and electricity grids began to fail, no one knew how to fix them, and when the oil and gas pipelines slowed to a crawl, national revenues dried up. No one else was trained to work as a domestic policeman or take care of other basic administrative duties, and the country literally fell apart into chaos. Further, many of those fired military forces of the Saddam Hussein government became inductees strengthening ISIS, which created a secondary regional disaster.

My point is that trying to recreate from scratch an energy infrastructure to accelerate the rise of renewables is not necessary and likely disastrous: almost all of it exists already and, for the most part, the energy companies and their supporting world own it, singularly know how to operate it, and have run it efficiently for decades. We 'only' have to make them want to use it to promote cleaner and sustainable fuels as they do oil.

I am an environmental advocate and have one message for my environmental friends: You are going about this all wrong in one critical way. Instead of working to starve oil companies and make them go broke, you should be helping them make incredible oil profits. Now, just stay with me a minute. I know this idea strikes against the instinct to punish oil companies. But, if you're looking for the fastest conversion to sustainable energy from fossil fuels, the quickest route is to make solar and wind more competitive, or even better, far *cheaper* than oil and natural gas. If that happens, you wouldn't need to help sustainable energy development with hard-to-get and hard-to-keep government tax credits and rebates, or beg for philan-thropist investments in smart grids, or try to make mothers feel guilty for not buying an electric minivan to take their kids to soccer practice instead of the Chevy Suburban they already own.

Instead, people will begin to actually *demand* solar power for their homes and run to buy EVs because they'll both be so much cheaper to use. Believe me, that'll make things happen in a hurry. Everyone wants to save money, and they will move heaven and earth to do it, trading in their gas guzzlers and nailing solar panels to their own roofs. Even climate-change deniers will do so if the discount is big enough.

There are two obvious ways to cheapen alternative energy compared to fossil fuels. You don't have to make solar, wind, geothermal, hydrogen, and the like much less expensive. You can accomplish the same thing, and do it easier if you make oil relatively far *more* expensive. One solution frankly relies on innovation, which you cannot predict. But the other relies on the capital markets, which respond predictably, given the right inputs. If you're looking for a green future, as soon as it's possible, then you want oil to cost a whole heck of a lot more money to get out of the ground, and you'll want it to stay really expensive to buy, literally forever.

Unfortunately, that's not been the history of oil prices, that's for sure.

With my strong advocacy for high oil prices, my environmen-tal friends might want to depict me as little more than an oil industry shill. In fact, the vast majority of my criticism for the mess we're in has been reserved for U.S. oil companies.

The multi-billion-dollar mistakes of mismanagement and poor timing of the U.S. LNG markets described above are dwarfed by the criminal waste committed by U.S. oil companies to the truly magical opportunity of horizontal drilling, or fracking for oil and gas here, in the last 20 years. The enthusiasm that first surrounded the U.S. "fracking boom" in the aughts and early 2010s was all well deserved. Here was a new technology that promised huge new supplies of oil and natural gas from land areas that were long thought to have been drained and barren. Recovery costs were relatively cheap compared to other types of oil and gas production, and with every passing year, they only got cheaper. The scaling of fracked wells was far easier than other oil and gas production as it required only a few million dollars of an initial investment to frack a well and get going. Domestic fracking held out real potential for U.S. 'energy independence' from foreign oil, which politicians in Washington had prioritized for decades. Finally, fracking as a new oil and gas source was uniquely possible in only a few areas around the globe. Of the very, very few significant shale "plays" that might yield quality and quantity of both oil and gas, the United States holds the vast majority of them.

What I'm laying out to you is a once-in-a-millennium opportunity that should have resulted in spectacular gains by investors, the U.S. economy, and the oil companies themselves. Instead, the insane drilling boom of fracked wells, using far too readily available credit, destroyed not only the prices and profits in the U.S. market, but the global market as well with surpluses from a new American ocean of fracked oil. Instead of learning from this mistake when the first bust of oil prices hit in 2014, U.S. frackers doubled down, increasing production even more and adding both to the glut and their already untenable debt-ridden balance sheets.

The bottom line is that instead of becoming one of the best investments, U.S. oil and gas instead became the worst-performing sector in the S+P 500, flushing trillions of dollars of capital down the drain. Further, the damage caused by the mad rush to frack wells has left toxic tail ponds, leaking pipe-lines, wasted vented and flared natural gas, abandoned drill sites, and a dozen other lesser but no less significant environmental problems. This sovereign, limited, and very valuable natural resource of fracked oil and gas has been literally pissed away, and no one besides the bonused executives of these oil companies have benefited much from any of it. Initial job gains have now become horrendous job losses; there have been hundreds of bankruptcies; and oil riches have been squandered and emptied for small or too-often-negative profits.

This should make you mad, as it does me. These oil and gas riches should have been ours, to benefit our American economy and not exclusively for the benefit of oil companies. I have watched for years as energy companies and even the energy markets themselves have slowly become bankrupt, and I am convinced that oil companies can no longer be trusted to manage by themselves these vital resources that we all rely upon. State agencies have proven incapable, and we need some stronger national guidelines on how and when oil and gas can be taken out of the ground and sold, for the benefit of our environment, but equally for investors in the oil companies themselves.

If the goal is a rising oil price in more regulated energy markets, there are only a few important players that we'll need to learn about. I've already given you a quick look at our domestic situation, both in the oil patch and in Washington; but the third player at our poker table is no less important: OPEC and the newly added associate member to that cartel, Russia. In this book, I've simplified OPEC and refer to Saudi Arabia often with near equivalence. That's because the Saudis are by far the most influential member of the cartel, with their overwhelming 11+ million-barrel-a-day supply.

There's plenty to examine inside the politics of OPEC, and it's fascinating. But for the most part, it's unnecessary here. The Saudis have dominated OPEC policy for years and generally get what they want inside the OPEC cartel. Since the oil bust of 2014, that's primarily been the pursuit of a successful roll-out of their Vision 2030 initiative. We'll be talking a lot about it in the chapter covering Saudi Arabia.

You've now been briefly introduced to all the players in our 'game': U.S. oil companies (and their Wall Street enablers), the environmental lobby, Washington, and the Saudis (with Russia a most interested bystander). All of these players have agendas that sometimes agree with their counterparts but more often are grossly opposed. We'll try to figure out where these goals have met, where they've diverged, and how to get this admittedly complicated train back on track towards a logical evolution towards renewables—a train that has recently come so far off the rails.

In doing so, we'll try to figure out how to "Turn Oil Green."

CHAPTER 1:

THE RENEWABLES CHALLENGE

H ow can we turn oil green?

I expect that many people who pick up this book might be rifling through the table of contents and the index, looking for the lone insight they came here to get, and I'm not going to be cagey about it. I have found through my nearly 40 years of observing energy markets that those markets do more than "make" prices; they also impose decisions on all of us. And those decisions, of course, are based on money.

While this is no surprise to anyone, it does create, for me, the surest way to chart a much faster and practical course towards renewable energy. Here's the simple insight: Energy users are far more likely to reach for the cheapest energy they can find that will do the job. That's easy, right? We'd all prefer to fill our tanks with dollar-a-gallon gas and wish that our electricity bills were as small as possible. Meanwhile, energy companies are going to spend their time getting and selling the most profitable energy they can find. For them, if sunshine and wind power makes them a better profit than mining tar sands oil and carving coal out of the ground, they'd be as enthusiastic about renewables as any environmentalist.

WHAT'S BARRING THE WAY TO RENEWABLE ENERGY SOURCES

The major hurdle I've seen to moving the U.S. towards renewables—in the way that it has happily and quickly moved in the past from wood to coal and from coal to oil—has been precisely this: Oil prices have stayed shockingly low compared to just about every other financial asset, and particularly since the oil bust of 2014. Renewable sources have been unable to compete with mature fossil fuels that remain the easiest and by far the cheapest energy sources available. Renewable sources have been getting cheaper all the time and have begun to honestly compete with oil in several places, but in a world dominated by fossil fuels (and the oil companies that profit from them), we need to find ways to push the timeline forwards as fast as we can. And there's one sure way to do it: First, make oil prices stable, and then consistently rising, like nearly every other asset class in the world. The stock market has its ups and downs, as does real estate, but you would be a very disappointed investor if your portfolio of stocks, or your house, were worth the same as it was in 2000, like oil.

Figure 1.1.
Oil Prices 1970-2020 (adjusted for inflation)

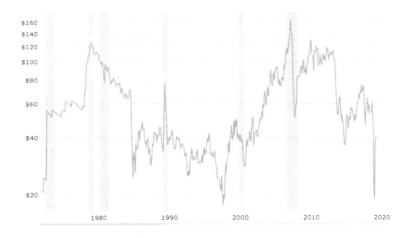

Adjusted for inflation, oil today is cheaper than it was in the 1970s (see Figure 1.1). Since the domestic shale oil boom starting in 2010, most of that weakness can be blamed on the mismanagement of this new domestic resource, by oil companies, Wall Street financial 'enablers,' and an inconsistent U.S. energy policy. Environmentalists have made the conversion to renewables harder at times—and not easier—by villainizing fossil fuels en masse and advocating an unpractical immediate end to all fossil-fuel extraction and use. This has placed energy companies as enemies of conversion towards cleaner fuels and renewable sources, instead of giving them a role—the most important one—of distribution and sale of these new energy sources.

All the chapters that follow this one will be (I hope) an interesting recount of how the world, under U.S. leadership, found its way into this mess, where we are today, and where we need to go to move the planet faster towards a greener and more sustainable place where humans are able to thrive for many hundreds of generations to come. It will explain some history of the world of energy and try to fathom some of the complex systems that drive the current energy markets. When you finish this book, I hope you won't be nearly as confused about oil, natural gas, solar, and wind power and why we're having such a tough time, collectively, in moving towards green energy and combating climate change.

There's a reason why you need to delve a bit into the history, and the current state of energy markets, so don't roll your eyes quite yet. Inside the understanding of modern energy markets lies the most important point in understanding how high oil prices can really make the conversion to renewables much faster. Those markets' sole job—establishing price—is the singular engine that incentivizes energy, in all its forms, to be collected and then delivered to consumers. I cannot stress this enough, and I beg you to keep that idea foremost in your mind as you continue on: PRICES DRIVE CHOICES. In any energy future that we want to craft, the first and foremost factor we'll need to consider are the costs and potential profits of energy in all its forms, and in all cases, the modern energy markets have by far the most important role in setting those prices.

The current crop of globalist thought leaders who comprise the Occupy, anti-Davos, anti-World Bank point of view are adamant that markets, including the energy markets, are the substantive problem that continues to drive power and wealth into fewer and fewer hands, and that this is what is causing the destruction of our planet through unredressed climate change. Of the symptoms they will say plague our global economy—the continuing poverty, resource scarcity, and unresponsive governments beholden to the rich—they will tell you that markets, and our global (capitalist) reliance on them, are in fact the disease. They will tell you that any solution that relies on the markets to be implemented will by its nature be flawed, taken advantage of, and turned around to benefit the few and the rich and not the vast majority who depend on universally accessible resources to food, water, and energy in order to survive and progress. In short, they will be suspicious of any solution that uses the capital markets as a gateway.

I obviously disagree. My life has been spent engaged on a daily basis with energy markets, trying to understand their causes and effects, efficiencies, inefficiencies, and their vast power to choose where resources are spent. I've seen many examples when markets have caused intense pain, delivered inequitable results, and benefited mostly those with the money to engage with them, while ignoring the vast majority of folks they are supposed to serve. But I've also seen incredible advances in the procurement, transport, and distribution of energy of all types, all of which could not have been accomplished without the vast capital allocation resources only made possible by modern energy markets.

With that 35-year history in mind, I'm going to argue that the system of modern markets that has developed over the last century and a half is not only an established vehicle for accepting and working inside the current status quo, but the only logical one to turn to if we seek practical change. Attempts at dismantling (or at least defanging) global markets and energy markets with them, particularly during the last financial meltdown in 2008, have proven that they do not bend and break easily.

Just the observable fact that capital markets have indisputably been proven to be incredibly resilient during times of crisis is not enough, I suppose, to guarantee their potential in effecting the global change we're looking to see, although I think that's a good start. But I'm also going to argue that markets remain the best independent source of information we have to assess the climate change issues we face and will be by far the quickest way to address them. Further, I believe that any change to the way we approach fossil fuels and renewable alternatives that we can sanction in a practical way using the capital markets will necessarily be by far the most universally accepted, both by those without money and power, but frankly by those with it as well, even if those solutions are very radical indeed.

I'll give you a quick example: Coal. Despite the tremendous initiatives of the Trump administration and his EPA commissioner and Energy Department secretary to "turn back the energy clock" and re-incentivize coal with various regulation rollbacks and FERC initiatives, coal usage continues to wane in this country on its way to what most agree will ultimately be oblivion. Nobody survives forever fighting the markets, whether they are rich or poor, in power in government or not. And if those energy markets point to a green future as cheapest and the most profitable alternative out there, if they continue to point the natural progression of energy towards solar, wind, and geothermal, and away from carbon sources, there is no one who can refuse to ultimately accept it.

I'm going to argue that if the world can be saved by higher oil prices, it is through markets that those higher prices need to be realized, and through those markets that our transitions to more planet-friendly energy sources will almost surely take place. I'm going to argue that we simply don't have the time to develop another system with the far-reaching ability to change our present circumstance with respect to climate.

RENEWABLES CAN'T COMPETE WITH CHEAP OIL

OK, all that said, how can higher oil prices, realized through the modern, established energy markets, push us towards a renewable future?

Well, let's start by taking a look at one of the most interesting charts from Lazard's last cost analysis of energy, from November 2017: Figure 1.2.

Figure 1.2.
Cost of Renewables vs. Fossil Fuels

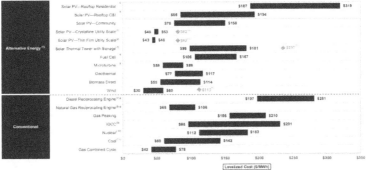

- 19 -

Here's a great study to begin to understand the financial environment of electricity markets in the U.S., where most all (renewable) alternative sources of energy are currently focused. Electric generation for home and business use is where we'll concentrate for the most part because it also encompasses the potential of electric vehicle (EV) use. Transportation is a smaller but still significant source of carbon output (about 31% here in the U.S.), so any moves that can be made away from gasoline-powered cars will be a major step forwards as well. But for now, let's try to keep it simple.

At the top of Figure 1.2, we see several alternative energy sources and the ranges of what Lazard calls "levelized costs" for each—basically, the dollars per produced megawatt hour with (nearly) everything taken into account. Where this analysis misses costs isn't really important now, but here's what is: You can see certain types of renewable sources of energy, particularly utility-scale solar and wind challenging both coal and natural gas on costs—something that has only begun to happen in the last several years. You can get a further sense of just how deeply these costs have been cut in only the last 9 years by having a cursory view of Figure 1.3, also from the same Lazard study:

Figure 1.3.
Dropping Costs of Wind and Solar Energy

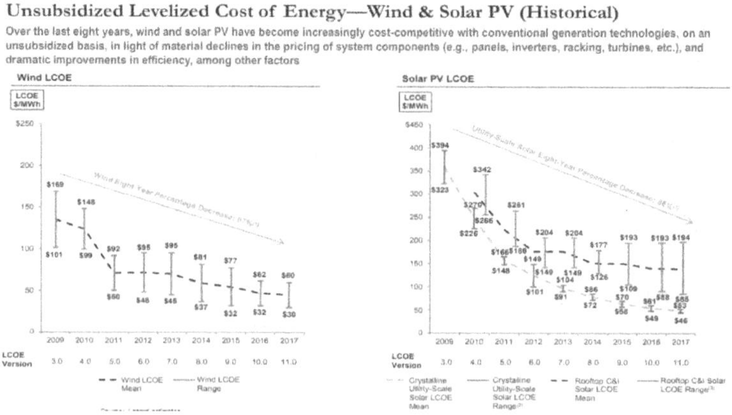
Unsubsidized Levelized Cost of Energy—Wind & Solar PV (Historical)
Over the last eight years, wind and solar PV have become increasingly cost-competitive with conventional generation technologies, on an unsubsidized basis, in light of material declines in the pricing of system components (e.g., panels, inverters, racking, turbines, etc.), and dramatic improvements in efficiency, among other factors
Wind LCOE
LCOE $/MWh
Solar PV LCOE
LCOE $/MWh
2009 2010 2011 2012 2013 2014 2015 2016 2017
LCOE Version
3.0 4.0 5.0 6.0 7.0 8.0 9.0 10.0 11.0
Wind LCOE Mean
Wind LCOE Range
Crystalline Utility-Scale Solar LCOE Mean
Crystalline Utility-Scale Solar LCOE Range
Rooftop C&I Solar LCOE Mean
Rooftop C&I Solar LCOE Range

As Lazard notes in Figure 1.3, wind and solar have become increasingly competitive to conventional, carbon-emitting generation. Costs have continued to drop from technological advances as well as increasing scale of use of both alternative energy sources. This is very good news.

So, if costs do continue to drop in green generation, gaining even more ground on traditional generation, doesn't that mean that dirty fossil fuels are ultimately doomed?

Not really.

I'll get into why that is later, but for now, let's hold in our mind the major positive for reduced global use of fossil fuels we've established already: Costs for solar and wind generation are trending downwards and getting more and more competitive with carbon burning (of all types) every year.

This is great, exactly what we want: Alternative energy sources like solar and wind are gaining on their carbon-burning competitors and in some cases overtaking them in cost—the most important trend we'd like to see to move us towards renewables. While costs for both wind and solar drop, however, the path of both graphs should be familiar to any student of high school calculus. They seem to indicate that costs are reaching their 'zero' limits quickly, and future discounts are certain not to be as spectacular, or as deep. It seems that both wind and solar are reaching their limits on their ultimate 'cheapness' rather quickly. We need to admit that the gains to be gotten from making solar and wind more competitive, by making them cheaper, are quickly reaching their limits.

Further, even with the competitive advances we've already seen in solar and wind generation costs, we haven't seen a very fast or wide-scale conversion from fossil fuel use here in the U.S. so far. It even seems that the inroads for really aggressive growth that has marked solar and wind generation in very 'green' Europe have begun to rapidly slow recently. Far from supplanting fossil fuels, renewable sources are not even managing to grow at the pace that global energy demand is increasing, leaving that shortfall still for oil and other fossil fuels to fill. And that increased demand for oil is not projected to slow any time soon. Globally, the demand for oil is projected to only go up until 2040—as shown in Figure 1.4—at least according to the International Energy Agency (IEA) as well as other sources—this, despite several "New Policy Scenarios" of clean energy adoption policies in Europe and the U.S., including the return of the United States to the emission agreements of the Paris Climate Accords.

Figure 1.4.
World Energy Outlook (WEO) Oil Demand Forecast
"New Policies Scenario" (NPS)

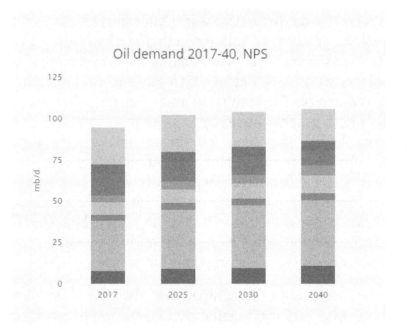

Oil demand 2017-40, NPS

There are a lot of reasons why oil is projected to continue to be in ever higher demand and currently remain so dominant in our energy mix for the foreseeable future. But the one that is most important to the future speed of integrating renewables is undeniably oil's relatively cheap cost. That's become more and more apparent as the oil markets have continued to swoon since 2018 and further drop because of the coronavirus pandemic. Low oil prices are destroying the competitiveness of wind and solar and scuttling environmentally sustainable technologies and their advancement everywhere I look.

I'll quote one that arrived in my inbox just this morning in August 2020. NRG Energy has just decided to 'mothball' its Petra Nova carbon sequestration plant. This flagship project for reducing carbon emissions through capture was hailed when it first went online in 2017. It was a combined effort of the U.S. Energy Department, which delivered a $190m cost-sharing grant to help its success, but even governmental support couldn't keep it alive in the face of low oil prices. I'll quote from the statement that was released:

> "Earlier this spring when oil prices fell, we ceased operations at Petra Nova and the delivery of CO_2 to the West Ranch Oil Field," NRG spokesman Chris Rimel said in a statement. "The carbon capture facility has been placed in a mothball status to allow it to be brought back online when economics improve."

Translation: We can't make money in carbon capture when oil prices are this low. The truth is, it's a lot tougher to make money in any sustainable technology or energy source when oil prices are low, and look to remain low.

IS PUSHING RENEWABLES THE ANSWER TO GETTING TO A RENEWABLE FUTURE?

 OK, let's recap. We've got markets telling us some very good things about the potential to get more green here in the United States, Europe, and several portions of the emerging markets, including China and India: Our primary sources of completely renewable energy—wind and solar—are becoming more and more competitive to fossil fuels, and those costs continue to drop, although they seem to be approaching their ultimate "cheapness" limits. It's great that they're getting cheaper, but clearly that hasn't been enough to move either the electric grid convincingly away from oil, coal, and natural gas, or to cause a huge turnover of automobiles from gasoline to electric power.

What could help us do that?

We've already figured out why merely making solar power competitive to coal, oil, and gas hasn't been enough to push us smartly towards a green future. But even without analyzing this any more deeply, what would we think intuitively would be the best way to push energy companies into more quickly abandoning their models for fossil-fuel procurement and sales, and substituting models for renewable energy procurement and sales? (And believe me, oil companies have been preparing for this swap for decades.) If that's tough to guess at, let's try this: What would push you from your Ford F-150 truck into one that uses Compressed Natural Gas (CNG)? Or what would push the commuters and mothers from their daily grind of driving to work or driving their kids in their Chevy SUVs into using battery-powered vans?

Well, what if gasoline had a national average cost of about $7.50 or even $10 a gallon, while CNG (compressed natural gas) could be bought for the equivalent of $1.50? What if an electric van, despite its reduced range, could be charged over-night for $0.75 for the equivalent gallon of gas?

And what if you KNEW that these relationships of oil being expensive and natural gas and electricity being cheap were not only going to remain, but get consistently wider—with oil go-ing up, up, up—while renewable sources continued to move down, down, down.

Sound impossible? No, in fact, it's truly the natural progres-sion of energy prices I'm talking about here—a progression that's been sidetracked by other forces in the last 10 years, forces that can all be understood, harnessed, and moved out of the way.

What if we could, through the current modern capital markets, move all of those forces back and out of the way, and allow the markets to define oil prices in their most natural, almost bio-logically evolutionary progression, where they continue to move inexorably upwards, towards $100, $150, even $200 a barrel? What would happen then?

You can understand and see the results as clearly as I. First, if it's really, really expensive to burn oil, people would obviously want to burn less of it, and only when they really needed to. If you were thinking of taking a recreational road trip to a campsite 350 miles away, you'd be more likely to consider the campsite that's only 50 miles out of town, even if it were less nice. Or if you were commuting every day into the city, taking an hour each way to go 20 miles and burning 3 gallons of gas in the process, you might consider a carpool or even a mass-transit option. If you're burning oil to keep your house at a toasty 70 degrees, you might think about turning the thermo-stat down a degree or two, or even finding another source of heat for your home—maybe one of those new-fangled solar water heaters or even some rooftop photovoltaic (PV) panels. No matter where you'd look, you'd see an enormous incentive to find ways to use less oil, and you'd get an enormous drop in CO_2 emissions—a tremendous and substantial environmental benefit.

Further, alternatives to oil become increasingly compelling, and this is not only in regards to renewables like solar and wind power that are our ultimate goal. First and foremost, with oil prices skyrocketing while other energy prices are staying stable, you'll get a fast conversion from oil to natural gas. The ability to easily substitute natural gas for oil in many of the ways we use energy makes this conversion a real no-brainer. In both commercial and individual use, natural gas is an easy swap: the move towards it on the electrical grid would be accelerated, while natural gas cars and trucks might finally take hold here in the U.S. And, in terms of carbon emissions, natural gas is a 50% improvement on oil and refined products, another substantial environmental gain. On the road to zero emissions, natural gas is the undeniably perfect 'next step' along that path.

We already have a market that has several trends pushing us towards a renewable future, with the continuing competitiveness of solar and wind power compared to other more traditional fossil fuels. But merely lowering the prices of renewable energy sources has not been enough to get us where we know we must be.

We've also got a far cleaner and more energy-efficient fossil fuel, in natural gas, that literally cuts our CO_2 emissions in half. But again, the movement away from oil and towards natural gas, at least in this country, has been hampered by the stubbornly cheap prices that we're seeing now in oil and refined products, and tend to revisit for various reasons every few years. Oil prices have seen boom time after boom time, when triple digits seemed to be the order of the day, and prices in the $50 a barrel, $40 a barrel, and even $30 a barrel range did not seem possible to be seen ever again. But, like clockwork, they always do come back again, stifling the progress towards natural gas and ultimately the zero-emission, sustainable renewables that we've been hoping to see dominate.

But if solar and wind costs and efficiencies keep dropping, and if we can be assured that natural gas prices will also stay relatively stable, we can finally move towards the future we're all looking to achieve merely by seeing oil prices rise—inexorably—above $100, toward $150 and $200 a barrel. Push the prices of oil up while keeping the costs of other sources low, and you'll supercharge the movement towards cleaner and ultimately zero-emission alternatives.

All of this incredible movement towards a green future, done not through boycotts of oil company stock, protests at the World Bank and Davos, national carbon taxes, alternative energy incentives, tax rebates, or wishful thinking—but through our already established capital markets and their mechanisms. Get the price of a barrel of oil to go higher and remain higher than other alternative energy sources, both renewable and not, and you're on your way to a clean energy future.

Not that these other measures of social and political change don't have their place in pushing us towards a more sustainable planet; they certainly do. But nothing, NOTHING, will get us closer to the ultimate goal of zero emissions more quickly than seeing the price of oil go up. Truly, higher oil prices can save the world.

Now, all we have to figure out is how to do that.

CHAPTER 2:

NATURAL PROGRESSION OF ENERGY

I n Chapter 1, I tried to outline all of the vast benefits we might see from a higher price for oil—a price that not only goes up, but STAYS up, relative to renewables and other, more eco-friendly carbon-based fuels.

Now, you might be an environmental advocate who has spent your entire life villainizing energy companies, working to restrict their profits, writing "BLOOD FOR OIL" on placards and taking them to marches, advocating a cut on oil company exploration subsidies and tax write-offs. You naturally think that high oil prices mean high profits for oil companies, and you are viscerally opposed to them in every way.

I understand well where you're coming from, but your instincts are incredibly and unfortunately wrong. HIGH OIL PRICES AND HIGH OIL COMPANY PROFITS ARE WHAT WE WANT as environmentalists. I've spent the last several years of my media life running around to TV and radio shows, podcasts, and other media outlets, telling everyone who'll listen that the natural instinct of trying to starve energy companies of profits and keep oil prices low is exactly the *opposite* way to get to the green future we seek.

We want the oil companies to succeed. In fact, we want them to succeed WILDLY: the more profits, the better. We want them to pursue big profits, because pursuing profits is exactly what motivates their behavior, better than any incentives or disincentives we can legislate or regulate. Much quicker than policy, it is a loose dollar bill that will get oil companies to move fast.

We've figured out that high oil prices will make natural gas and renewables far more competitive than they are right now. And competition from natural gas and renewables will naturally cause end users of all kinds to want to use less oil and other, cheaper, and greener fuel sources. Competition from cheaper alternatives also drives profit margins. If you're taking oil out of the ground for $80 a barrel and selling it for $120, you're making a 50% profit on your money: not bad. But, if you're taking natural gas out of the ground for $2 per mmBtu and selling it for $4, you're making a 100% profit. That's twice as good. If you can develop a wind farm and amortize the cost so that you're spending $0.03 per kWh to make electricity, and then you're able to sell it to the grid for $0.09 per kWh, that's a 300% profit. Now we're talking.

Think of that incentive on oil companies, too. Sure, in our new-market world of high oil prices, oil companies would be doing better by drilling and providing oil at $120 than ever before, but even then, they'd much rather sell natural gas and make twice as much, or develop electrical energy alternatives and make six times more. The oil companies themselves would become the biggest advocates for an accelerated conversion to natural gas and alternatives, both for heating and transportation. In this way, the markets that we reserve so much suspicion for can ultimately drive our environmental goals forwards, better than any tax or regulation might.

MARKETS ARE NOT UNCONTROLLABLE

So, at this point, I might have convinced some of the more hard-core left-leaning thinkers about the immense power of the marketplace to do good for people and help, rather than hinder a green energy future, given the right conditions. There might even be a few of you who are ready to jump all-in on board with the idea of using the power of the markets to dictate policy, as opposed to the other way around. But, even if you're prepared to be the kind of unicorn liberal who thinks like a capitalist (like me), you'll still come up with one very big question in all this:

Sure, maybe high oil prices would be the market condition to steam us globally towards cleaner natural gas and renewable energy sources, but how do you control the markets?

If anythin ... *But how do you control the markets? Socialism?* 10 years, and certainly you'd have to say that t le, but highly uncontro ets to move a certain w er, but that's kind of a p.p. u.uu., isn't it? Isn't oil just another capital asset, like any other stock or bond or commodity, and therefore as easily likely to move up as down?

Well, maybe in the short-term that's right, but in the long-term, the answer is most definitely *no*.

What if I told you, even without asking the markets to do a thing for us, that it is "natural" for oil prices to move continually higher anyway? Start with this: The costs to explore and recover crude oil all continue to spiral upwards as new sources continue to get deeper underwater, more buried underground, and require more and more specialized technology to access. The easy sources of oil we've all relied on continue to dry up, and new, less easy sources of oil get more and more expensive to find, access, and develop.

You also probably already know that oil is a limited resource, an idea commonly known as "peak oil theory." We won't get into it much, but it's important to recognize that like death and taxes, the ultimately limited nature of fossil fuels is an incontrovertible fact. We're unlikely to ever get close to that limit, at least if we're not going to see a concurrent massive rise in global temperatures and the destruction that will come from it. But, even if we never get close to the limit of our collectively limited oil resources, what's important is that the costs of finding, drilling, moving, and using that oil get more and more pricey the closer we come to that limit. In other words, the pressure for oil to go up in price is a natural cause and effect from every barrel of oil that currently gets used, every single day.

And it's not just new sources of oil that get more expensive; the remaining cheap barrels already being pumped get more expensive as well. That's because oil is priced globally, whether it comes from Saudi Arabia, Nigeria, Russia, or the United States. They all refer their prices using the cash and futures markets in London and in New York. Using those markets, every barrel of oil that comes out of the ground, no matter where it comes from, is priced using the same market mechanism, and to a greater or lesser degree shares a relatively equivalent price because of it (besides some geographical and grade differentials). That market mechanism is known as "marginal barrel pricing" and is a very important concept we will need to understand fully. For now, it's important to remember that if we need to find more and more expensive oil to fill ever-growing global energy appetites, it is not only the new barrels that are more expensive; EVERY BARREL of oil gets more expensive.

Let's recap for the moment. Oil is running out, if very, very slowly. Oil companies, since the beginning of their business, have drilled for oil in the cheapest places first. In the hundred years since, those 'cheap' barrels have been slowly but inexorably running out, and the barrels found to replace them (keeping in mind that the demand for barrels continues to increase), get more and more expensive. This is what I mean by a natural upwards progression of oil prices.

MARGINAL BARREL PRICING

Oil comes out of the ground at different costs for every well that's drilled. It changes depending not only on where it's coming from, but how it's being taken from the ground. You probably already know that the costs for getting a barrel of oil out of the sands of the Saudi Arabian desert are a whole lot less than getting them from 2 miles down in the Gulf of Mexico. Now, oil comes in varying 'grades' and the prices that different grades receive are definitely different, but all of them are tied to a global benchmark price. But if the costs of recovery vary so much around the world, how can the markets come to a simple, one-price benchmark for pretty much all oil, everywhere?

That's what we call pricing the 'marginal barrel' of oil.

Let's try an analogy.

Let's imagine that the Mott's corporation needs 100 apples a day to cover the company's daily demand for making applesauce, and Mott's is the only buyer of apples—in other words, Mott's represents the entire demand of the market. Let's also suppose that Mott's doesn't really care what it pays for those apples, because the company can easily pass those costs (along with its profit) onto a public that will pay whatever Mott's charges. In our apple world, let's say that eating 4 ounces of applesauce a day is absolutely essential to maintain good health and has become a necessary cost for people, even before I-phones and Netflix subscriptions. (In economics jargon, we'd call this an inelastic demand – just like oil.)

Let's also say there are only three apple farmers: one in Washington, one in New York, and one in Michigan. Our Washington farmer spends 10 cents to harvest an apple; in New York, it's 20 cents; and in Michigan, where the weather is less conducive to apple growing, it's 40 cents. All of our farmers make 10 cents profit per apple just to make it worthwhile to stay in the apple growing business.

What should 100 apples cost Mott's?

Well, if Mott's can get them all from our Washington farmer, the company will spend $20 (10 cents costs + 10 cents profit X 100).

But let's say that our Washington farmer can provide 50 apples a day, at most, depending on how much of his orchard he decides to plant, while both our New York and Michigan farmers are capable of planting and delivering 30 apples a day each. Now what should the apples cost Mr. Mott?

Now, we've introduced another issue: we're dealing with a glut supply. Mott's now has access to a total of 110 apples, even though the company needs only 100. Still, what should the Mott's Corporation pay for the 100 it currently needs?

The answer is $50: it is the cost of the most expensive apples that Mott's will have to buy in order to satisfy its demand, applied to ALL the apples the company will have to buy.

You'd think it wouldn't work this way, but let's examine why it has to: To fill the company's daily need for apples, Mott's buyer goes first to the Washington farmer and contracts to buy all of his 50 apples at 20 cents apiece. (50x20=$10). Mott's buyer then goes across the country and cleans out our New York farmer for his 30 apples at 30 cents each. (30x30=$9). But now, Mott's buyer must go to the last source of supply, in Michigan, to buy the last 20 apples the company needs to complete its demand, paying 50 cents apiece in order to reach 100. (20x50=$10). It would seem that Mott's should have paid a total of $29 for those 100 apples. Why did I say that Mott's total bill would instead be $50?

It's because the apple market is an open market, just like oil is – and no Washington farmer in an open market is going to sell his apples for 20 cents when some other farmer in Michigan is getting 50 cents for his. Similarly, our New York farmer has no reason to discount his harvest in an open market either. In open market pricing (like oil market pricing), it will always be *the highest price* paid to satisfy the *TOTAL demand* that will determine the price that EVERYONE is going to charge for their goods.

Let's make a few quick parallels between our imaginary apple market and today's oil market, and U.S. shale oil barrels in that market.

The current oil market that's been glutted since 2014 by shale oil production has a worldwide demand of more than 100 million barrels a day. Most of that supply is being provided by what we'd call the "Washington State" producers, who can get oil out of the ground for relatively little cost (Middle East, Russia, and other OPEC producers). But these barrels are not enough to supply the full amount of global demand by themselves. Our Michigan farmers (currently, U.S. shale producers) provide the last few million barrels that cover demand fully, and their costs are far more than most of these other suppliers. This is why the growth of U.S. shale oil of 3 million barrels a day in the last 5 years and nearly 10 million barrels a day since 2009 has been enough to completely control the pricing of the entire global oil complex, despite being merely 3% of the total supply.

Figure 2.1.
The Recent Dominance of U.S. Shale Oil on the Global Oil Markets

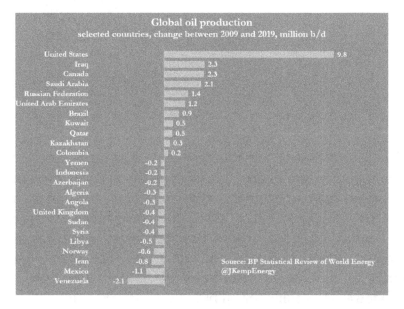

If oil prices should move higher 'naturally,' what's stopped it? Now we're getting to the heart of the matter. It is the growth of U.S. shale oil, shown in Figure 2.1, that has made the natural upwards progression of oil prices impossible, and you've certainly figured that out if you've been watching the oil markets at all in the last decade. We've seen prices move from a pretty steady area between $20 and $40 a barrel during my first days of trading oil in the '80s to take off during the years from 2003-2008, reaching a high of over $140 a barrel. Then, the financial crisis took oil down again below $30 in 2009, only to recover as the global economy did, to bounce above $100 a barrel for a few years between 2010 and 2014.

Figure 2.2.
U.S. Shale Oil (tight formation) Production, (2005-2018)

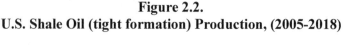

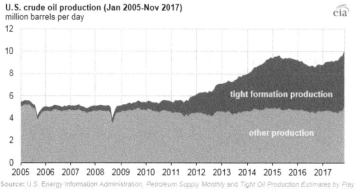

Right at that time, a new source of oil was being developed and soon came to dominate domestic production in the United States, as shown in Figure 2.2: Shale oil from horizontal drilling, known as "fracking." What had started slowly in the early part of the century exploded, with a new "shale revolution" creating dozens of new oil companies, all falling over each other to pump oil and take advantage of $100+ oil prices. From 2011-2014, that rush towards fracking for oil brought U.S. production from under 6 million barrels a day to over 9-½ million barrels a day, truly testing the entire global supply chain for oil. Singlehandedly, that production explosion created a glut that caused another price collapse, this time again to near $30 a barrel. Since then, oil prices have been only slowly recovering, briefly reaching near $70 in 2018, but never really threatening triple digits again, as in 2006 and 2011. From an outsider looking in, with little or no experience with oil or the oil markets, you'd have to say that there is no natural progression for oil prices, or at least there isn't one that's been very reliable.

And boy – would I have to agree with you there. Except underlying all this, there is.

I'm going to spend a lot of time in Chapters 3 and 6 talking about all the hurdles that oil has been forced to jump through to get back on its 'natural' path towards higher prices in the last two decades. It's a story of missed opportunities, Wall Street excesses, and oil company greed. Frankly, as a witness to this vast corruption and mismanagement, I've kind of enjoyed the comedy show, a real entertaining lifetime of really, really bad decisions inside the industry and even worse policy ideas from Washington. Maybe it's a joke only I get, but I'm going to share it all with you and see if you can laugh alongside me.

Meanwhile, and for the sake of getting you on track with the thesis of the story, I want to leave you with the most important central idea to take away for now: Oil prices should naturally and steadily increase.

THE EVOLUTION OF ENERGY SOURCES

One more point needs to be made in this fast overview of energy history, before we move on to get a bit deeper into the weeds of where we are in our energy plans today and where we should be headed tomorrow—another natural progression that cannot be ignored, away from coal and oil and towards natural gas and ultimately low and zero-emission renewables.

I want you to start thinking about coal, oil, and all the other energy sources you can think of as you would stages of any other evolutionary chain. That is key to understanding what I believe are the 'natural forces' leading oil prices higher, and oil utilization lower.

Figure 2.3 shows a pretty famous, simplified image of the various stages of human evolution, from Chimpanzee to Modern man.

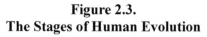

Figure 2.3.
The Stages of Human Evolution

Seen even in this very, very inexact representation, you can see a natural progression of posture, bone structure, height, and other proportions. Maybe it's because we've seen this kind of picture over and over in our lives, or maybe because, like the frames of a movie, it's almost intuitive, but the progression is satisfying and needs little outside information to comprehend and believe. One moves understandably from one image to the next, and it's difficult to imagine, for example, that modern man could emerge directly from the Cro-Magnon man represented three stages earlier. No, each stage is necessary, and small changes must take place before bigger changes are possible. Evolution in stages is clearly the 'natural' as well as the most efficient way towards progress, no matter how slow that progress ultimately takes, as with the millions of years for human evolution from our ape forebears to where we are today.

Such is the way to think about global energy production and use, as shown in Figure 2.4.

Figure 2.4.
A Projected Evolution of Energy

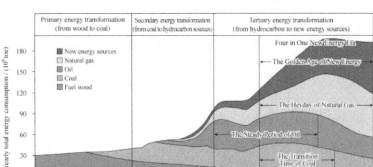

Figure 2.4 was created by the research division of the Chinese state-run oil company PetroChina, and it does a super job projecting the progression of global energy evolution in exactly the same way as the famous one you know well of human evolution. The first important point from Figure 2.4 is to show how logically energy sources 'build" on their predecessors. No new source is able to immediately or completely 'wipe out' its predecessors, but merely augment and add to it, at least at first, as its precursors slowly lose their dominance and fade. It also equally shows a 'natural' progression of energy sources, beginning with wood in the earliest parts of the 19th century and seeing its first competition and beginning conversion to coal around 1850, when we see coal use begin to slowly cut away at the predominance of wood. You don't need to be an energy scholar to guess how or why coal was able to begin to eat into the market for wood: It quickly became a cheaper and more efficient source of heat and power—easier to transport and store and delivering more energy release at a lower cost.

Also in Figure 2.4, we see coal continue its ascendancy through the 1920s, when oil and gas are first commercially drilled and commercially developed. The difficulties of corralling and transporting natural gas in the early part of the last century naturally led to an easy choice and reliance on crude oil, the other product of fossil fuel drilling, which as a liquid (or semi-solid) has obvious advantages in the early part of the 20th century.

By 1970, crude oil has become the dominant energy source, contributing nearly 50% of all global energy supply. Already, we can see clearly the outlines of three stages of our 'natural progression' of energy: we're at a sort of equivalent to the 'Cro-Magnon' stage for energy from the previous example, with oil leading the way as coal and wood continue their natural declines downwards, decreasing in importance to the global energy mix. By 1970, pipeline systems are better established here in the U.S. and globally, making natural gas a more accessible source of energy: remember when your father questioned whether to change his home boiler to natural gas from heating oil (a crude oil product) in the '70s and early '80s?

At this point, oil companies can truly make complete use of both fossil fuels emerging from the same drilling process and work to gain equal ascendancy for their 'other' fuel, natural gas. There are several advantages to the fuel which we'll get into, but most important from an historic point of view, natural gas requires little to no processing, and can go to your local utility or your home water heater nearly in the same state as it flows from the wellhead. Dramatically cutting the costs oil companies must shoulder to make their raw product into a consumer-usable one makes natural gas potentially far more profitable than crude oil and a real comer in the energy mix. Even in its early stages of distribution, with oil companies pushing the fuel because of its advantages of profitability, natural gas quickly gains in global demand from 1970 to 2000, eclipsing coal in a mere 30 years.

Since 2000, however, the further 'evolution' we've come to expect in energy (as with our own human evolution) has begun to exhibit some 'weird' characteristics. If all were going normally, we'd expect the efficiencies of oil and natural gas to continue to extinguish the demand for wood and coal, and in many ways, that's exactly what we've seen in the 20 years since 2000. But we'd also expect the efficiencies of natural gas to inspire a rise towards complete ascendancy just as all the previous stages of energy before it, from wood to coal to oil. Eventually, we'd expect natural gas to eclipse the other three as the world's preeminent energy source, and that's what the researchers also seem to expect in Figure 2.4. But what I see are several roadblocks preventing that progression that are standing in the way. Although that chart has great promise for the ultimate dominance of natural gas and then renewables, I continue to have my doubts. There are many, many reasons for us to have seen a wider swap already, besides the profitability of natural gas to other energy sources. We'll talk about all the reasons that hasn't happened in Chapter 10.

But for now we merely notice that the ascendancy of natural gas has not yet occurred, despite being well supplied, and in many cases over-supplied here in the U.S. With all of its advantages, one would really expect natural gas to have rocketed to the top of the energy food chain already: It's cheap, plentiful, burns more efficiently with 1/3 the emission artifacts of crude oil, needs no processing, and is far more profitable, when managed correctly. Yet, surprisingly, here in the United States, natural gas still accounts for only 29% of our total energy consumption by source, as shown in Figure 2.5.

Figure 2.5.
U.S. Energy Consumption by Energy Source, in 2017

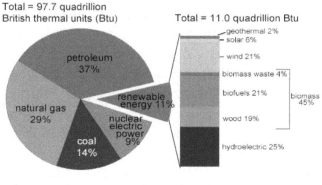

U.S. energy consumption by energy source, 2017

Total = 97.7 quadrillion
British thermal units (Btu)

Total = 11.0 quadrillion Btu

petroleum 37%

natural gas 29%

coal 14%

nuclear electric power 9%

renewable energy 11%

geothermal 2%
solar 6%
wind 21%
biomass waste 4%
biofuels 21%
wood 19%
hydroelectric 25%

biomass 45%

Note: Sum of components may not equal 100% because of independent rounding.
Source: U.S. Energy Information Administration, *Monthly Energy Review*, Table 1.3
and 10.1, April 2018, preliminary data

eia

In order to reach again the 'correct' progression of energy sources we're looking for and move us quickly to a sustainable future, we're going to have to work to fix this. I'll talk about a few practical suggestions that I believe will work both with the market forces we want to exploit and the practicalities of politics in Chapter 11. But for now, let's look at the next obvious stage along our timeline towards the energy equivalent of modern man: the ascendance of renewable sources like wind and solar.

(By the way, don't get too excited by Figure 2.5 if you're a fan of renewable energy. The 11% of total energy consumption of renewables above includes our old friend, wood, at 19% still more than three times larger on a percentage basis than solar, at a mere 6% of 11% of the total. That's right, as of 2017, solar is still less than 1% of total energy consumption here in the U.S. We've obviously got a lot of work to do.)

We've already seen the relatively fast drop in costs for PV cells and their competitiveness to other electrical energy sources.

But we've got to expect that truly sustainable renewables like solar and wind power will only reach their ascendance and dominance in the global energy mix by using the same 'natural' evolutionary mechanisms as we saw with coal, oil, and are far too slowly seeing with natural gas. Just as we wouldn't expect modern man to emerge directly from an ancient ancestor like the Cro-Magnon, so we shouldn't expect our sustainable future to emerge from whole cloth by policies that advocate the complete abandonment of fossil fuels. Instead, we should expect increasing costs for the former to begin squeezing out the old technology for the new and forcing the competitive mechanisms of the market to 'naturally' advocate for renewable energy.

That's why the outlook I've seen overwhelming taken by environmentalists has confused me and been, in my view, completely opposed from the one most likely to achieve the goals they're after. If you're an environmentalist, you're not an advocate for the banning of fossil fuel drilling and the divestiture programs that look to starve oil companies of capital. Instead, you'd be a very strong advocate for anything that will send oil prices higher—and you're going to counter-intuitively want to see oil companies make a very strong profit on oil sales.

Further, you're going to want to see natural gas assume its natural, evolutionary role as the transition fuel between oil and renewables. Whether you are an oil executive or a full-blown, tree-hugging advocate for a completely fossil-fuel-free and zero-emissions future, your best route to that goal is going to be to work to accelerate the rise of natural gas usage, as the next logical step forwards—another step towards the end of our evolutionary ladder, dominance of zero-emission renewable energy. With that, we will have arrived at our energy equivalent of modern man.

I know that's some strange brew to swallow, if you've been on the opposite side of recent fracking wars in natural gas heavy states like Ohio, Pennsylvania, and New York. And we'll discuss the problems with fracking natural gas as well in Chapter 10, without apology or spin and try to figure out where the risks of natural gas fit in with the rest of the world's energy demands. They exist, they are plentiful, and they need to be dealt with just as they do with oil production.

For now, however, let's try to get our arms around the idea that renewables will become a dominant source of energy and fuel our green energy future only when they can fit in the natural progression of energy sources, which don't eliminate fossil fuels but first supplement them before supplanting them in the energy mix. This is the kind of natural progression we've witnessed since the first moments that man put a commercial use to burning wood to keep himself warm and forge rudimentary tools.

If we're looking to honestly move the ball forwards towards a green future, we all have to become advocates for and create policies that will help create a rising price of oil and a growing dependence on natural gas.

So let's take a look now at what has hindered that progress, that should otherwise have already happened, as I say, 'naturally.'

CHAPTER 3:

U.S. SHALE: HOW SO LITTLE MEANS SO MUCH

W e can't help but make a pretty deep-dive analysis into the monumental surge of crude oil production we've seen in the last 5 years from the United States, and specifically from shale formations in the Dakotas and West Texas, if we're to understand where we've been and where we are going with oil. I committed another book (*Shale Boom, Shale Bust*) specifically to describing the activity we had only begun to see there when I wrote it in 2015; since then, there has been a greater surge in activity than I (or anybody else) could have possibly imagined back then. That book was written to try and understand the part that U.S. shale would play in the global supply chain for oil and possibly try to predict some investment opportunities that might have played out since.

For this book, however, we have a different need in mind. Of the many hurdles that oil prices have tried to overcome to find their 'natural' path higher in the last 7 years, none has been more significant than the inexorable (and frankly, self-defeating) increases in production that have come from U.S. shale producers. More than any other reason, this massive increase in oil production not only initiated the bust cycle of oil prices we saw in 2014, but has been integral in keeping the prices of oil low (at least relatively) as of this writing in late 2020. Whereas oil prices have seen triple digits on a fairly steady basis, first before the financial crisis in 2008 and then after 2010, we've instead remained doggedly and substantially below that $100, and even an $80 threshold since 2014, as you can see in Figure 3.1.

Figure 3.1.
Inflation-Adjusted Price of Oil (1990-2020)

No one could argue that the most significant impasse for oil prices regaining those higher levels that we've seen over the last 15 years represented in Figure 3.1 was the collapse of global growth and shortage of corporate credit that accompanied the financial crisis of 2008-2009. But that moment in financial history was (we hope) surely an outlier. During that time, not only oil but the global economy at large came off the rails in a way we haven't seen since the Great Depression of the 1930s, certainly a most uncommon economic event. Seeing oil prices under such duress not only sink below $80, but even approach $30 signaled—at the time—a global economy that was on the brink of failure, and required massive and unprecedented government intervention from the United States Treasury to avoid reliving a most dark economic period of the 1930s.

But now look again at Figure 3.1: since 2014, we've been seeing similar depressed prices for oil we've only seen before in 2008. And, in stark contrast to that global crisis, there's been no shortage of credit, nor anything but an increasing global demand picture for oil. We've actually seen the opposite: fairly robust global economic growth in that time period, at least in the United States and China, which are still by far the two largest consumers of oil.

In no way have there been the kind of monumental systemic barriers to economic health that we saw during 2008-2009, nothing to even approach the recessionary pressures and slowdown of credit we saw then. Quite in contrast, particularly in the oil space, credit has been in fact overflowing and easy to find, a fact I'll talk quite a bit more about in Chapter 6, concentrating on U.S. oil fracking. So, when I say that the biggest hurdle to higher global oil prices since 2014 has been U.S. shale production, I'm not kidding around: without the increased U.S. oil supply inputs from shale, oil prices should have—in my mind—almost certainly already surpassed $100 a barrel. We would have never experienced the price collapse we saw in 2014. And further, we would have likely made new highs by now to compare to the incredible oil spike we saw in 2007, nearer to $150 a barrel—if not more.

GLOBAL DEMAND FOR OIL CONTINUES TO INCREASE

We hardly need to be advanced economics students to come to this stunning conclusion, as even the most cursory analysis of the simplest supply and demand numbers will prove it, as shown in Figure 3.2.

Figure 3.2.
Global Oil Demand (in million bbls/day)

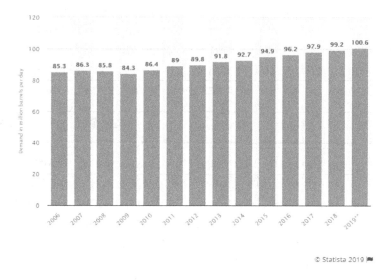

© Statista 2019

For example, since 2014, demand for oil globally has increased by nearly 8 million barrels a day, a stretch of tremendous oil demand growth, even by historic standards. A benchmark I have always used to mark a period of 'normal' economic growth for oil, starting after the OPEC embargo in the 1970s, has been an increase in demand of 1 million barrels a day per year. Through the '80s, '90s, and 2000s, oil demand growth has been fairly steadily following this pattern, with obvious variations on the downside during periods of recession and upside increases during very robust growth.

In contrast, the period from 2014-2019 has shown more than an average 50% increase on our 1-million-barrel-a-day-per-year benchmark—indicating this period as being a globally very robust economy indeed. But has it been? Is there an economist in the world who would put the U.S. economy during this recent time anywhere near on par with those we've experienced through the Reagan or Clinton years? Our current GDP of 2-3% over the last several years is dwarfed by the growth rates of the '80s and '90s. In Europe, certainly, there can be no argument that recent GDP growth has been flat and often negative since the 2008 crisis, and even in the fast-growing Asian economies, most would argue (including me) that we've not seen the super-hot growth of earlier in the century.

With all this said, one need not wonder where the price of oil would be if U.S. production had stood still during that time. Demand growth of such a robust rate, even in these times of relatively steady global economic activity, should not lead to depressed prices for oil at all. At the very least, we should not be looking at prices that are at least $40 lower than where they were prior to 2014. In all cases, we must look at the only factor that has significantly changed to figure out why oil prices haven't responded positively to such intense economic calls for more and more: the immense rise in U.S. oil production since around 2012.

Just how significant has the boom in U.S. oil production been? Let's look at the numbers, and again, a pretty glaringly obvious chart to show them, in Figure 3.3:

Figure 3.3.
U.S. Oil Production Since 1985(millions of barrels a day)

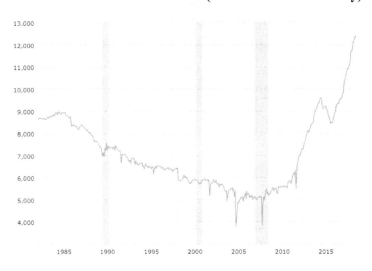

We're going to concentrate specifically on the impact of shale production on the global supply of oil, and I'm pulling out Figure 3.3
from microtrends that go back well before oil from shale was ever
a significant contributor to U.S. supply for a reason. Before we can
understand the massive impact U.S. shale oil had on upending the
'normal' trends of global oil supply, we need to see where U.S. production was headed before shale oil ever came on the scene. Figure 3.3 does that perfectly.

The first trend to point out, which is so important to understanding our story, is the natural decline of U.S. oil production that had
begun and been the trend since the 1960s. "Old-style" conventional land-based oil production that dominated in the U.S. until
recently is the type that most folks commonly think of when they
imagine oil coming out of the ground: a rotating derrick with a
drill bit that moves in a straight line downwards, probing for pressurized veins of oil that, once released, come flowing out under
their own pressure. Maybe in their minds, folks see a Wallace
Beery or John Huston-type character, overseeing and dancing
around a gushing well like the one shown in Figure 3.4:

Figure 3.4.
Old-Style Land-Based Oil Drilling

For decades, this image (in Figure 3.4, of Spindletop in the 1920s!) was how oil production in the U.S. was perceived. What's even more interesting is that, despite the many modernizations of pipe constructions, geological technologies, and fancy gauges, this "conventional" method of oil production was a pretty accurate representation of how most of the oil that reached the marketplace through the late 20th century took place: through rig derricks and vertical drills. Even today, conventional oil production is still a major source of the global supply chain for oil, overwhelmingly the norm in the Middle East.

What's important is that the trajectory of oil production in the U.S., as you can see in Figure 3.3, had continued to move decidedly downwards since the 1960s and even more rapidly downwards throughout the rest of the 20th century and into the first decade and half of the 21st, as conventional wells in Texas, Oklahoma, Alaska, and California, among others, continued to run dry. At the time, this was a trend that was considered unchangeable—oil from the United States was on a clear, predictable, and unstoppable path towards zero—and oil companies and oil-producing nations were planning their capital spending, exploration, and future production based on this apparently inevitable trend.

Multi-national oil companies had always had partnerships outside the U.S. for foreign sources of oil, and those arrangements were responding to lessening U.S. crude supplies by getting larger and more far-reaching; for example, with Exxon and BP in Russia. Middle East nations, Russia, Nigeria, and other African and Mideast National Oil Companies (NOCs) all expected to be the dominating sources for oil in lieu of the dying volumes coming out of traditional onshore wells in the United States. Moreover, not only did those new supplies need to supplant an onshore U.S. supply that was continually decreasing, they needed to deliver it to a world market that was also significantly increasing its demands for oil every year.

A systemically decreasing supply in a marketplace that continued to have ramping demand? That's a very simple recipe for a very sharp, steady, and mostly unstoppable spike in oil prices. And in energy circles, that's exactly what was expected. Before 2014, almost every oil analyst on the planet with any knowledge of the energy world (including me) was predicting oil prices that would likely never see anything other than triple digits, and was further expecting even more violent spikes, perhaps even above the incredible prices we saw before the financial crisis of 2008. Triple digits, combined with systemic supply shortages and prices approaching $200 a barrel (and more!) were considered by most experts to be the inevitable trajectory for oil.

If not for the revolution of pressurized fracturing of underground shale formations, otherwise known more generally as *fracking*, the 'natural' order of increasing prices, and the also natural progression we've posited that would have flowed towards other sustainable and renewable energy alternatives would have certainly moved much further along globally, and not stalled as it currently has in (relative) insignificance. That's how important the 'shale revolution' has been to global oil supply, and ultimately the slow global pace towards sustainable alternative energy sources.

I'm not equipped to give a long explanation of the geology or physics of fracking, the unexpected source of all of this new oil and natural gas. For our purposes, you only need to know how fracking opened up a previously unconsidered and enormous reservoir of new fossil fuel supplies. Instead of mostly vertical wells taking oil out of large underground pockets under their own pressure, fracking moved smaller and multiple 'fingers' in between layers of shale, using a pressurized cocktail of water-based fluids to 'stimulate' the rock into releasing the oil and gas hiding there.

There are three critical milestone implications that this new technology had on oil supplies that need to be discussed:

- first, the enormous amount of new oil reserves that shale added to the global supply chain;

- second, the many financial implications of the world's prime shale formations being found overwhelmingly in the United States;

- third, and perhaps most important, the relatively cheap costs and short-term investment associated with shale fracking, as opposed to most other modern oil production methods.

THE REVOLUTION OF SHALE OIL

Applying raw numbers, the U.S. largesse of shale oil (on its face) does not seem all that significant. As of 2016, proven reserves of U.S. shale (a difficult number to rely on to begin with) was estimated at about 40 billion barrels. This is against a world-wide reserve of approximately 1.7 trillion barrels of (supposedly) recoverable oil. Given this ratio of a little more than 2.5%, U.S. shale reserves don't really seem very significant, certainly not enough to upend the entirety of the global energy marketplace—which, I hope to show you, they have definitely done. But, these numbers are more than a little deceiving, because all oil isn't created equal.

The two most important metrics to understand when valuing any oil reserve are what grade of oil we are considering and how much it will cost to get at. Oil is graded using many metrics, but the most important is its sulfur content. And sulfur content is an easy one to understand: The more sulfur in the oil, generally the less valuable it is. Sulfur is a useless contaminant that requires expensive processing to remove, so the more sulfur, the more expensive it is to turn our crude into oil products that people can actually use, such as gasoline, jet fuel, and plastics.

Now that we have a little (very little!) context into types of oil (there are actually dozens, even if we normally only refer to one or two), let's have a look at Figure 3.5, showing the relative world-wide reserves in regards to sulfur content.

Figure 3.5.
Reserves Broken Down By Sulfur Content

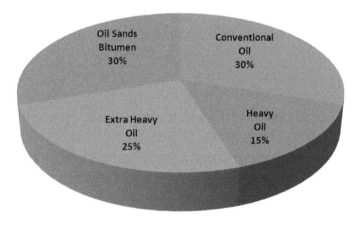

Total World Oil Reserves

You'll find the lowest sulfur content in what's referred to in Figure 3.5 as 'conventional' oil (not to be confused with conventional oil production), although in the industry, it's more commonly called 'light' or 'sweet' oil, and that's how we will refer to it from now on to avoid confusion. Sweet grades of oil can be found in Nigeria, in the Gulf of Mexico and other off-shore sources, and yes, it is also produced here in the United States onshore from both conventional wells and non-conventional shale formations.

As you proceed clockwise around the pie chart in Figure 3.5, you find increasingly higher contents of sulfur, referred to as 'heavier' grades. For example, Saudi oil is a generally heavy grade of crude with more sulfur than U.S. domestic grades and won't be worth as much on open physical markets as are other 'sweeter' oils. You'll see Saudi grades of oil trade on oil exchanges at something like a $4-$10 per barrel discount to sweet crudes.

As we proceed around the pie chart in Figure 3.5, we get to oil sands, the heaviest, almost rock-like form of oil that is so thick it is more often mined than drilled for. Oil sands reserves, for example, are a significant part of Canadian production in the Athabasca area of Alberta.

The processing costs for oil sands, because of their heavy, sulfurous quality, are very expensive; therefore, this grade of crude oil naturally brings the lowest price on the open market in its raw state. Western Canadian Select (WCS—which is the Canadian oil sands benchmark) often trades at more than a $25 discount per barrel to the United States 'sweet' 'light' benchmark, West Texas Intermediate (WTI).

Venezuela has by far the largest reserves of heavy oil sands in the Orinoco, but they are deeper underground and much harder to get at even than those in Alberta. Because of the added costs associated with the mining, transport, and processing of these reserves, and considering the wide discount that oil sands suffer from, it is currently uneconomic for anyone to commit significant resources to getting them out of the ground. Venezuelan oil sands are so expensive to access and process that some analysts predict that these huge and potentially valuable assets might never be accessed. That's a lot of oil we're talking about there, by some estimates as much as 270 billion barrels, nearly equal to all the other sweet conventional oils reserves in the world combined. The oil sands of the Orinoco alone account for nearly 16% of the world's previously noted 1.7 trillion barrel reserves. Even at $20 a barrel, the potential value of these Venezuelan oil sands is over $5 trillion (!!) dollars, and knowing the current financial state of Venezuela, the people there could certainly use some of that, but will more than likely never see much of it, ever.

That's how important sulfur content is—that, and the ability to get it out of the ground and to market. These are the two main metrics, then, that will tell you most about the real value of any oil reserves we're going to talk about, sulfur content and cost of extraction.

For business folks, whether they're in oil or not, there's obviously nothing that takes much precedence over profits. So, with the knowledge you've just gotten about global oil reserves, it's pretty simple to guess where oil folks are going to look first for the oil they want to sell: They're going to prefer sweet, low-sulfur grades of crude oil that will return the highest premium in the open market. Besides that, they're going to want to sink the least amount of money they can in getting that oil out of the ground, in order to maximize their profits when they get that oil to market. It's a simple equation: the highest-quality, lowest-cost oil you can find is going to be the obvious first choice of every oil company who's got a choice to make:

- Can I stick a pipe in the ground with an old-fashioned oil drill bit, or do I have to pay to rent a multi-billion-dollar drill rig sending pipes and other expensive equipment remotely down into three miles of water?

- Will I need to coax the oil out with sophisticated pressurized cocktails of gases and liquids, or will it come out under its own pressure once tapped?

- How much money do I need to spend on service extras like advanced hydraulics, cementing, environmental disposal of wastewater and rock, and engineering and worker expertise?

- Once I get at the oil and it comes to me, do I have to transport it through extreme weather over hundreds of miles to get it to market?

- Or can I put it in a ready pipeline for an easy 200-mile ride to a major tank center at a major port?

- Once I get it there, how will the marketplace value my oil? Will I get $20 a barrel? $40? $60?

- How fast is that price apt to change and what can I do to make sure I'll get the price I planned for when I started drilling?

If you're an oilman doing your crucial math, those metrics are the main ones you're going to use to decide where you're going to devote your very precious capital resources.

Finally, once you've made your calculations and made your choices, you're going to want to stake that claim for as long as you can and plan to drill and exhaust those resources for as many years as you can, before you have to move along and spend money developing another, likely less profitable source of oil elsewhere.

All of that is true, that is, if you HAVE a choice on where to go and get your oil. Saudi Arabia, in contrast, doesn't have much of one: its resources are limited to its own domestic reserves (although it has recently begun investing in other foreign sources of oil, including shale!). Even today, its domestic conventional reserves are immense and nearly as easy and cheap as the old-fashioned Spindle Top example I showed in Figure 3.4, which have long since run mostly dry here in the United States, yet continue to flow in the Middle East. Even today, the costs of getting conventional Saudi crude oil out of their desert sands rarely goes above $10 a barrel, and cheap costs like this are pretty much the norm in other countries that make up most of the rest of OPEC as well. Therefore, for the Saudis, the discounts that heavier grades of Saudi crude suffer in the open market are more than made up for by the cheap costs and easy access that the Saudis and other Middle Eastern nations have.

U.S. and European mega-cap oil companies like Exxon-Mobil, BP, Chevron, and Shell work in a different world than the sovereign oil-producing nations in OPEC. These companies aren't limited by their own national reserves to explore for and produce oil. They have choices all over the world of where to go for oil, and for the last century, they have often chosen to engage with foreign countries for oil procurement. For them, the metrics remain the same, however: find the cheapest oil that can be sold for the greatest premium, wherever that oil may be.

I'm not able to give you (and you're probably not willing to read) a long presentation of mega-cap oil capital expenditures planning and considerations. But when a big oil company gets involved in an oil deal in a foreign country, there are other things to be considered besides the simple costs of getting that particular oil out of the ground and the return when it gets to market.

Certainly, the leasing arrangements are foremost. Most countries want a nice 'first cut' of profits from any oil that comes out of the ground in their sovereign land, although many oil analysts will tell you (as will I) that oil companies have historically done very well in keeping these 'cuts' relatively small.

They are able to do this because many third-world nations simply don't have the technology or ready capital to get their oil harvested and processed themselves, and often need the advanced technology and experience of the multi-national oil majors. They often have little choice but to accept the rather tough terms that oil majors offer in order to access their own reserves. It also doesn't hurt that the leaders in many of these third-world nations are often corrupt and apt to take a personal incentive of their own to accept a perhaps more lopsided arrangement.

But even with favorable leasing terms inside a foreign land, there are other dangers for oil majors in foreign countries to consider. In the Mideast and Africa, geopolitical strife is often a fact of life, and civil skirmishes to outright wars are not uncommon. Rebel and terrorist disruptions, disease, the added costs of employing and sending trained drill teams, mechanics, and engineers to faraway lands—all of these translate into costs that become part of the calculus when embarking on a project in a foreign country. There is also the risk of U.S. government or even military action that limits the business or trade that oil companies can do abroad, or the ultimate risk of an election or regime change in that foreign country that refuses to recognize previous contracts, repatriating assets and leaving oil companies with nothing to show for their investments but a plea to very weak international arbitration. We've seen recent cases where some very big investments from oil majors came to disappointing ends: for example, with BP in the Russian Arctic and U.S. sanctions spoiling Exxon's investments in Russia as well.

All this to say that, on balance, and all other variables being equal, oil majors would most certainly prefer to do business here in the U.S., or at least in countries that have a quiet geopolitical outlook, well-established business interests with other Western companies, and a legal system that can be relied on.

All of which makes that 40 billion barrels of U.S. shale oil reserves look mighty good indeed to oil company executives.

WHY U.S. SHALE OIL IS SO DESIRABLE

I've said that the quality of the oil and the ease of getting at it is what oil folks care about. Now we are better able to see why U.S. shale oil has become such a hot commodity, moving quickly to the top of the priority list for many large and small oil companies:

- Firstly, all of that shale oil is right here in the U.S. and is concentrated in 5 or 6 key states.

- All shale is an onshore resource, which doesn't require first going through water (sometimes a LOT of water) before the drill bit hits something solid, as offshore oil recovery does.

- Shale oil used to cost quite a bit to get out of the ground, but with recent innovations has become far more competitive to other onshore and offshore reserves.

- Finally, shale oil is a very 'sweet,' highly desirable grade.

That's a lot of positives for a comparatively small cache of oil reserves, and it's why U.S. shale oil is such a compelling investment for U.S. and other multinational oil companies.

Let's examine how those 'mere' 40 billion barrels of U.S. shale reserves have managed to upend the global supply marketplace, economically threatened OPEC and other oil-producing nations like Saudi Arabia, and derailed the 'natural progression' of energy towards renewables that we would have already hoped to have seen.

I must first remark that U.S. shale oil production remains dominated by smaller independent oil companies, although the majors continue to rapidly increase their influence. Chapter 6 is devoted almost exclusively to those independents, because their history and current state in the shale patch tells us everything we need to know about how we got to the current energy disaster we're examining and hope to fix. But first, we need to get the majors out of the way: Their growing appetite for shale oil is a critical part to any market-based suggestions we might have to actually fix it.

Companies like Exxon-Mobil, Chevron, Conoco-Philips, Shell, BP, and others have by far the most money and expertise of all the world's oil companies and are therefore uniquely able to get at just about any reserves that the world has on offer. So, just how hot are the majors to 'get in' on the shale revolution?

Chevron has a long-standing commitment to U.S. oil, sitting on acreage from as far back as the 1920s in West Texas, and its initial commitment to shale has been mostly a lucky one: large reserves were discovered on already owned, conventional holdings. With 500,000 acres in the super-hot Permian basin alone, it would seem that Chevron already had more than it could handle in U.S. shale oil, yet Chevron participated in a short war to buy out independent Anadarko Resources in the spring of 2019, offering a losing $48 billion for that company, a shale powerhouse that produced 266,000 barrels a day of U.S. shale oil in 2017. Despite that losing bid, Chevron found an even better deal to increase its shale footprint by buying Noble Energy for a far more moderate total of $13 billion in July of 2020, taking advantage of the coronavirus disaster in the oil patch to buy the shale independent at a vast discount. CEO

Michael Wirth has promised 900,000 barrels a day of shale oil by 2023, a promise that the Noble acquisition makes clear was no idle talk.

BP ponied up $10.5 billion for the U.S. shale assets of Australian mega-cap BHP Billiton in 2018; this after already owning significant shale assets in the U.S. and being a long-time leader in U.S. offshore exploration and production in the Gulf of Mexico. The combined holdings were then placed into a separate operating company, BPX Energy, as if to highlight the importance of shale to BP's future production.

Conoco-Phillips sold the entirety of its Australian oil and gas operations for $1.4 billion in 2019 specifically to concentrate on its North American shale plays.

But Exxon has likely been the most aggressive of the majors in acquiring unconventional assets in the United States. Under CEO Rex Tillerson, Exxon was the first major to make a large acquisition of unconventional acreage by acquiring XTO Energy, a shale independent, for a lofty $36 billion in 2009. This deal might go down in history as perhaps the worst oil deal ever, as XTO was almost completely engaged in the production of shale natural gas and not shale oil—and natural gas was about to embark after the crash of 2008 on a long-term downwards price spiral that continues today.

In retrospect, although Exxon certainly overpaid for XTO in 2009, the company has refused to admit its error (in any operational way at least), and the bones of XTO Energy have served as the base under which Exxon has continued to acquire more, far more oily, shale assets since. The biggest of these undoubtedly was the 2017 buyout of the privately held Bass family assets in the Permian shale region of New Mexico—a $5.6b deal that doubled shale reserves overnight for the company.

In recent oil industry conferences, CEO Darren Woods has indicated that Exxon might not yet be finished buying U.S. shale acreage, and has promised a million barrels of shale oil a day from the company by 2025. This would have an incredible impact on the company if Woods can manage it: as of 2018, Exxon produced a total of 2.3m barrels a day of all fossil fuel liquids, including oil. For what is still the largest U.S. oil company and fourth largest in the world, that 1 million barrels a day would represent an enormous percentage of Exxon's output and its tremendous focus to growing shale oil production—above all other offshore and international options—in the next 5 years.

The hunger of multi-national mega-cap oil companies to throw mega dollars at U.S. shale oil is stunning, making those 'mere' 40 billion barrels a major focus of the world's largest oil explorers. Yet the single most stunning aspect for me as a markets analyst is in knowing that these companies know a lot more about oil than I do, can go virtually anywhere in the world to get it, and yet are choosing to get it here in the United States. There are a lot of obvious reasons why this is happening.

First, this country is far more regulatory friendly than practically anywhere else in the world, particularly in oil-rich states that have a long history and tradition of oil extraction, such as Texas and Oklahoma. I'll talk quite a bit more about that and how the 'wildcatting' open-market freedoms that have dominated oil drilling might be altered to help push this country towards renewables in Chapter 11.

Second, there are no foreign interests that need to be catered to, no added 'incentives' needed to get favorable leasing arrangements. Privately owned land can be leased to oil companies with little restriction from the U.S. government, and some public lands are available in competitive auctions open to all. Contracts, when they are entered into, can be relied on to be adhered to, with the power of the U.S. court system to insure redress.

Finally, with the latest improvements in lateral drilling and spacing, new efficiencies in fracking management, fluids, pressures, and other technological advances and improving success in predictive geology of productive acreage, shale oil has immensely decreased its average price per barrel of extraction even in the short time that shale has become a significant contributor to U.S. oil supplies.

And here is the key to understanding the import of shale oil to the future of the U.S., and global supply chain: it's cost. Because while it's nice to have the support of local governments and courts in your search for oil, the bottom line is always profits – and U.S. shale oil has recently become very, very cheap to produce.

Further, profits are not only about what it costs to simply get oil out of the ground; it matters even more what you'll get when you try to sell it. And it's here we must devote serious time to the smaller oil independent companies we've so far passed over—the ones that started this whole shale-fracking boom, and who drove shale and global oil into the catastrophic price bust we've seen since 2014.

How did these guys screw up what should have been one of the greatest free-market capitalist stories the United States has ever seen?

How did they take a new and enormous resource that is the envy of every other country, and in ever greater demand

and—unbelievably—manage to bankrupt themselves totally in less than a decade?

How and why did they throw the balance of oil reserves so off-kilter that OPEC was forced into a strategy of self-destruction to try and stop them, and then force them to catastrophically reverse course after failing that?

And finally, how did the combined greed and mismanagement of independent oil companies and Wall Street team up to short-circuit our natural progression of energy towards renewables so completely that we're now playing catch-up on a global warming threat that looks very possibly to have already run away?

If we can figure this out, perhaps we can find some answers to getting ourselves back on track towards a sustainable energy future. Without that understanding, I believe we're just flailing in the dark.

CHAPTER 4:

SAUDI ARABIA AND THE FAILED PROMISE OF THE SAUDI ARAMCO IPO

O f all the players in our drama of oil prices, Saudi Arabia seems to me to be the least well understood, although the Saudis are, in fact, the easiest to figure out. Villainized by the press and held accountable for oil prices worldwide, the Saudis are held to a Western cultural standard they cannot yet approach and an economic standard they haven't yet reached. They are currently working harder than any other Middle Eastern nation to modernize, albeit slowly, their 15th-century traditional Wahhabi culture, while simultaneously trying to broaden their 20th-century economy away from oil. In both goals, the Saudis have only one possible fix: very high oil prices. And as the ostensible leader of the OPEC cartel, they are always working to assure the highest oil prices they can for themselves and their members. That is what a cartel does and there is nothing else for them.

But in pursuing higher oil prices, they've had to balance a U.S. government that has demanded restraint in oil pricing in return for military support to fend off religious adversaries in Iran and Yemen and secular adversaries in Iraq. Further, they've been met in recent years by a U.S. shale oil competitor that has stubbornly refused to curb its output, no matter what incentives or disincentives have met them in the marketplace.

Put together, this has left the Saudis in a constantly precarious situation. On the one hand, they are left to deal with U.S. oil producers, who want to take advantage of the Saudis' unilateral supply cuts and OPEC-wide quotas to move oil prices higher, while doing all they can to scuttle those efforts in the marketplace by flooding it with their own oil. On the other hand, they have been recently forced to answer to a current U.S. administration that is more obsessed with high oil prices than any other in the past and is willing to use every tool in its arsenal to deter the Saudis and OPEC from pushing them higher.

I was preparing for a well-deserved trip to Italy in the summer of 2018 when the news broke that Saudi Arabia was 'shelving' its plans for the initial public offering (IPO) of its state-owned oil company, Saudi Aramco. On the face of it, this was horrible: I had been looking for a three-bumper bank shot to drive higher the oil stocks that my subscribers to my advisory service, The Energy Word, and I hold—and the main leg of this stool keeping oil prices rising had been the prospect of a very, very successful Saudi Aramco IPO. Now that there were indications that this public rollout of the Saudi oil assets might not happen at all, I could have a major problem on my hands.

My clients' oil investments are the least of it, however. In the last several years, Saudi Arabia has been maneuvering slowly through the morass of Arab geopolitics, a bust cycle in oil prices, and a monumental change in the U.S. Presidency, all while trying to hold together its big modernization plan for the country: Saudi Vision 2030. Some might claim that this far-reaching document—which looks to change the Kingdom's approach to social and religious freedoms and the economic base that finances it—is little more than a public relations move by King Salman to push forward his young son, Prince Mohammed bin Salman, as the next ruling monarch (and an evil despot, at that).

I do not.

On the contrary, I see it as a first shot across the bow of traditional, conservative Arab politics and stagnant social progress.

PRINCE MOHAMMED BIN SALMAN – A NEW SAUDI DREAM

I know, I shouldn't even weigh in on this. Nobody really cares what I think anyway. But after the 35 years I've had following global oil geopolitics, it's hard not to look on the new Prince (a local rock-star figure now sporting the acronym "MbS") as a major shift in Saudi and Middle Eastern norms and a legitimate new hope for progress towards the 21st century from a region stuck in the 15th. But I know that, especially in light of the orchestrated and cold-blooded murder of *Washington Post* reporter Jamal Khashoggi, it becomes tough to see the new Saudi leadership as anything other than a further repressive evolution of a historically repressive, brutal religious regime.

Still, the outline laid out by MbS and agreed to by his father Salman in Vision 2030 is impossible to ignore: A grand proposal to remake Saudi Arabia socially, politically, and religiously and to bring the Kingdom into the modern era. Already the Prince has been slowly removing religious restrictions and allowing women to drive or take certain jobs without permission from their traditional male guardians. While we in the West tend to view these changes as piddling in a modern world, they are, in fact, major progressive steps for the Wahhabi Saudis. Restrictions on some Western culture distribution, including some U.S. films, have begun to be relaxed. Courses offered in the universities are beginning to have far more open scope. There are a lot of reasons to believe that Vision 2030 is more than just a proposal full of smoke, but a real step forwards towards freedom for the people of Saudi Arabia, and by effect, for those that have previously led them.

But nothing so motivates Vision 2030 as the proposals it advances for changing the economic status of Saudi Arabia, moving it from a singular, oil-based economy to a more diversified modern one. For all the newfound freedoms, the monochromatic economy leaves few opportunities for the youth of the Kingdom, which is a major problem because the median age of Saudi citizens is 29.8 years old. Ultimately, the purpose of Vision 2030 was born out of this demographic necessity: Find a reason for young people to live happily in Saudi Arabia, or be prepared for the problems that a young, repressed, and bored youth will inevitably cause.

The backbone of this economic transformation is the monetization of the Saudi oil assets, represented by the sale of state-issued bonds (the first of which was seen in 2018), but more important was the IPO of the state-controlled oil company in charge of the Saudi oil fields – Saudi Aramco. This is the super event that the oil world has been waiting for, and looked, at least in 2018, to be at least another year on the horizon.

Why? What put the Saudi plans on hold? And why is this IPO so important for us to know about, and even root for its success?

Of course, in the Saudi Aramco IPO, we're back to where we started and where we must always return: to the price of oil.

A BRIEF HISTORY OF MIDDLE EASTERN OIL

Let's do some very brief work on the importance of oil in the Middle East, without getting too deep in the long dynamic of Saudi Arabia and the rest of OPEC. A good place to start is the latest 'breakeven' prices for the Middle Eastern economies in regards to oil prices, shown in Figure 4.1.

Figure 4.1.
Oil Prices Needed for OPEC Countries to Balance Their Budgets

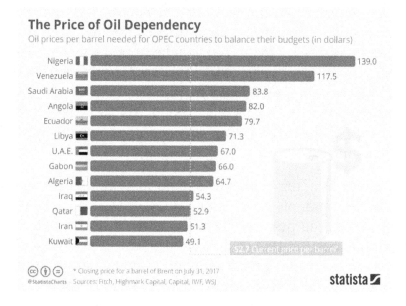

In 2019, the International Monetary Fund (IMF), the watch-dog of global banking, confirmed that an oil price of $80-$85 was needed to balance the current Saudi $300b budget. That is an oil price that has not been seen since 2014. Make no mistake, the crash in oil prices we saw then came as a shock to U.S. producers, but not least to the Middle Eastern countries whose entire economies rely on them to finance virtually everything for their citizens. We won't make a deep analysis of the crisis in Venezuela, but the dire current situation there was greatly accelerated not only by the oil collapse, but by the even more unexpected long-term discount in oil prices below $80 through 2020. You might ask whether the Saudis and other oil-reliant nations are getting panicky about the cash burn that their treasuries are enduring in light of low oil prices, and what these nations are actively doing about their predicament.

In the first case, there is indeed some distress, depending on who you are in OPEC. For Venezuela, low prices have caused a general panic, a government in chaos, and all the precursors of a civil war. In Iran, despite its equal reliance on oil revenues, its relatively low breakeven point to finance its restrictive and threadbare economy, as well as its restrictive religious government control has given Iran far more room to handle the distress of low oil prices. But what difficulties that remain have been heightened in the last three years by President Trump, who has scuttled the Obama/Kerry nuclear non-proliferation agreement, again cutting oil exports and oil revenues, a hardship that Iranians were only relieved of since May of 2015. We might note that the relief from these long-standing sanctions came as oil was experiencing its worst bust in prices since 2008, and the Iranian economy didn't recover significantly before Trump restored sanctions in 2017. For the Iranians, low oil prices have been a double whammy they continue to struggle against.

For the Saudis—where this ongoing budgetary shortfall is most important for our purposes—there are fewer problems from this relatively long bust cycle in oil prices than in places like Iran. That is not only because the Saudis have a large cash buffer that a decade of $100+ oil prices have delivered, but also because MbS, with his current cult status in Saudi Arabia, has relatively little political risk, even if he ultimately needs to suspend some social programs and lessen the current annual drain to the nation's sovereign wealth. But cutting programs, despite the current low price of oil, is certainly not what the new prince MbS seemingly has in mind.

Quite to the contrary, MbS's commitment to Vision 2030 becomes ever clearer as his plans for Saudi Arabia become ever more ambitious, despite the low global price for oil. In 2017, in the midst of this oil bust, the Prince announced plans to build a $500b mega-city where none existed before, on the coastline in the most northwestern province of Saudi Arabia. This city, named Neom, envisions fully renewable energy infrastructure and futuristic reliance on robots and even flying cars. The development director for this fanciful project that MbS named is a corporate 'rock star' in his own right, the former CEO of Alcoa, Klaus Kleinfeld. Its proposed economic zone of new universities, businesses, and recreational attractions was to be financed by the sovereign wealth fund of Saudi Arabia, with further funding by private investors. Daniel Doctoroff, the previous second-in-command to Michael Bloomberg, was an advisor on the project. These grand plans had to be scrapped as the outcry from the Khashoggi incident gained volume and Western potential investors and partners became more difficult to find.

But the failure of Neom points up not only the ever-more-ambitious and perhaps even unrealistic plans that MbS intends with Vision 2030. More important, it stands as an example of how the disappointments of low oil prices, combined with the murder of Jamal Khashoggi, have combined to dim the prospects for the Saudi Aramco IPO and the modernization of Saudi Arabia itself.

Why am I spending so much time on this offshore Wall Street deal? What the heck does the conversion of a state-run Arab oil company into a publicly traded one have to do with the prospects for renewable energy? I cannot stress strongly enough how much we all actually need a powerfully successful outcome for Saudi Aramco to further the hopes of a faster global transition towards renewables. I know it might seem that the prospects for the Saudis to find a big price for their oil isn't of much importance to us as promoters of a greener global energy future, but it most certainly is.

In the simplest terms, the ability to quickly change the total global oil supply on hand is still primarily in the hands of OPEC, more than anyone else in the world. And inside of OPEC, the Saudis are by far the most important force moving the cartel in its policy of regulating supply. Previously, the Saudis had a simplistic, parochial view towards how they regulate oil supply, using the needs to finance their own economy and the economies of their cartel members, but Vision 2030 forces on them a new approach they've not ever needed before. The monetization of Saudi Aramco changes their responsibility to their own economic needs and instead makes them responsible to shareholders and even more to the global capital markets at large. The long-term success of the rollout of this new public company is the fuel that powers Vision 2030; it alone can continue to finance the big, modern, and futuristic plans that Mohammed bin Salman has in mind for his country.

All of this will require even stricter controls on Saudi production, and to the degree they can, on OPEC production. Better controls on supply will equate—again—to a sustainable and high price for oil, which—again—is what we're after. So I'm going to continue to explain the story of Vision 2030 and Saudi Aramco to get a full view of what we can do to promote this ongoing goal of the Saudis. And that story continues with the ill-timed murder of Jamal Khashoggi.

THE TERRIBLE TIMING OF THE KHASHOGGI MURDER

Much of the media reported the murder of the *Washington Post* journalist Jamal Khashoggi as if that crime had been completely ignored by the Trump administration. I don't believe that was at all the case. In fact, I believe the Trump administration used the incident to pressure the Saudis into abandoning oil supply quotas, going into the midterm elections of 2018. Further, this tragic occurrence reached well beyond the political quieting of a dissenting voice in Khashoggi; it has worked to destroy the planned timeline for the Saudi Aramco IPO and limited its success. It is clear that the brutal murder of Jamal Khashoggi deserved global recognition and economic punishment, which under the Trump administration, it did not get. Still, the assassination, because of the negative impact to the Saudis' Vision 2030 initiative, has turned out to be by far the biggest mistake of the young Prince's fledgling career as the up-and-coming ruler of Saudi Arabia.

The Saudi-born Jamal Khashoggi was an ex-pat journalist living in the United States who had a history of writing uncomfortably negative columns about the restrictive, corrupt, and repressive conditions in Saudi Arabia. While visiting the Saudi embassy in Turkey to complete documentation to divorce his Saudi wife and prepare to marry his fiancée, Khashoggi was detained and never exited the embassy. Both CIA and other European intelligence agencies confirmed that Khashoggi was murdered while in custody there and that the murder was directed by the Crown Prince Mohammed bin Salman. It isn't normally a major story when the Saudis imprison or even execute one of their own, but this murder, done on foreign soil to a legal resident of the U.S. (working for a major newspaper), made major headlines.

It seems that Trump didn't waste the opportunity that the global pressure on MbS was providing. He sent Secretary of State Mike Pompeo to Riyadh in October 2018, yet he emerged from those one-on-one meetings with little to say about the circumstances of the Khashoggi death, except to say that the Prince was taking 'appropriate' measures to find those who had killed Khashoggi. Indeed, in late 2019, five men were ultimately sentenced to death in Saudi Arabia for the killing, without (of course) any blame for that circling back to

the Prince. When U.S. intelligence sources concluded that the
Prince was in fact the source of the assassination, Trump instead denied the finding.

But what did Trump and Pompeo get for this easy dismissal of
scrutiny from the United States? It has become fairly obvious:
A continued commitment from the Saudis to keep oil prices
low, at least through the 2018 midterms. Trump has been
caught out several times admitting to making such a transac-
tional agreement through his Secretary of State on numerous
occasions, saying that he has a 'direct line to the Prince' and
'he sends me oil whenever I ask him to.'

This is in direct contrast to the frustration that the President
often showed towards the Saudis prior to the Khashoggi incident in regards to oil prices, often tweeting his anger. With
prices near $80 a barrel in early 2018, the President de-
manded the Saudis release more oil and drop prices on several
occasions, once threatening that the U.S. might not militarily
support them otherwise. That back-and-forth skirmish between the President's Twitter account and the royal family
went on for months, with neither a concession from the Saudi
King about further supplies, nor a drop in oil prices.

But since the Pompeo meetings, in contrast, all has remained
calm, both between the President and MbS as well as with the
oil markets throughout 2018 and 2019. Here's a case where it
not only looks like a duck and walks like a duck; it sounds very,
very much like a quacker, too. There seems no other reason
that the Saudis would suddenly abandon what had become a
very successful curtailment of supplies and a subsequent very
broad price rally in late 2018, right in front of their planned
Aramco IPO.

Indeed, not so coincidentally, just after the Pompeo meetings
in October 2018, the Saudis temporarily abandoned their two-
year-old production guidelines that had spurred an oil price

rally that had begun in the Summer of 2017—a rally that had moved prices up more than $30 a barrel. When prices again dropped into the mid-$40s in late 2018, the Saudis hurriedly reversed this supply free-for- all. But the damage (or the U.S. quid-pro-quo) had already been achieved. Also not surprisingly, since that time, even though a new production ceiling has been maintained inside OPEC and with the Russians since that oil price fallout of 2018, we have not seen a sustained rally in oil prices to match those seen in the fall of 2018.

At least until the coronavirus struck, taking all control of oil prices away from the Saudis, OPEC, the President of the United States, and even God himself, oil prices barely budged outside of the $10 range between the high $40s and low $60s, seemingly 'keeping' the silent bargain that the Crown Prince made with Trump's Secretary of State. Until oil prices again reach a level that seems to bother the U.S. President, as they did in the fall of 2018, I suppose we won't know whether such a coincidental number of events related to the Khashoggi murder were in fact the unreported 'deal' I suspect happened between Trump and the Saudis—but if they do, it will be very, very interesting to see the President's reaction to them in the midst of his reelection campaign.

And what of the Saudi Aramco IPO? Since 2017, the IPO has hung very much in limbo, first announced as a grand $2 trillion roll-out, but ultimately emerged as a far less impressive event. Throughout 2019, the Saudis continued to push for a big IPO on a big exchange, either in New York, London, or Hong Kong. Every large investment bank was consulted, and the Saudis clearly hoped for an optimistic plan from one of them to give the Prince his big coming-out party—a hoped-for $2 trillion valuation on the New York or London exchange.

As the banks and the Saudis went back and forth during the summer and winter of 2019, it became clear that more than low oil prices stood in the way of MbS's big party: Major exchanges wanted far deeper due diligence on the professed Saudi oil reserves than the Kingdom had ever dared to provide anyone, and banks were therefore far less inclined to recommend an IPO price anywhere near the Prince's $2 trillion, coming in at less than $1.5 trillion, in several cases closer to an unacceptable $1.2 trillion.

The Prince has been left with some poor alternatives. He clearly remains under Trump's watchful eye with oil prices, having made an arrangement to keep prices below a certain threshold, at least until the 2020 elections are completed. Also, in light of the quick work he made of competitors inside the house of Saud, he needed to begin some delivery on the big promises of Vision 2030. He further was left with no international exchange willing to deliver the valuation he needed to validate the IPO to his satisfaction, but he also was running out of time to at least establish the company as a publicly traded vehicle.

Because of all this, he finally opted for a very small float IPO in Riyadh, using mostly local investors to keep the prices high, a disappointing first start for the major monetization he was hoping for and on which his long-term plans rely. For the time being, however, it will have to do. The partial IPO accomplishes all the Prince ostensibly needs, with its bloated valuation and at least partial monetization of $26b to begin to deliver on some of the promises of Vision 2030.

But ultimately, a much more accomplished sale of shares in the company is going to be necessary, from a far more diverse group of investors. And, again, there is nothing that will entice investors to come and buy shares in the Saudi oil assets more easily than a very, very high price of oil.

The Prince might have problem providing that right now, but with the knowledge of what his plans are, we can count on the Saudi Aramco IPO as being a very useful vehicle for gauging the progress that Saudi Arabia and therefore OPEC are making in our plans for a quicker transition to renewable sources.

SAUDI ARABIAN ENVIRONMENTALISTS?

It seems that OPEC and the Saudis would be the least interested in helping along the global march of energy towards sustainable sources, but in fact, it is the new head of Saudi Arabia, with his very forward plans for the reimagining of his country who is also very much hoping for the kind of global market that will make that happen far sooner than later. What makes MbS such an interesting and important figure in the global energy scene is his clear grasp of the inevitable future of renewable energy and his very deliberate efforts to get his country diversified away from fossil fuels as quickly as he can.

Yes: Mohammed bin Salman is acting as an environmentalist, and we must do what we can to help him be successful.

I know that I have been unrelentingly critical of all of our energy 'players' in this book, save for the Saudis and Prince bin Salman here. This may strike many as strange, considering that the Saudi Arabian kingdom has a long history of religious oppression, abuse of women's rights, a class structure that retains oil wealth in the hands of very few sheiks and princes, and with still very strong ties to the terrorists who comprised the majority of those involved in the 9/11 attack. The natural instinct is to view the Saudis as enemies of the U.S. and the U.S. economy – particularly U.S. energy companies. Indeed, outspoken shale company leaders like Harold Hamm and U.S. Congressional members have often taken advantage of this characterization to conflate that suspicion with U.S. shale's competition for oil market share. As we will see in Chapter 9, this is not a fair connection: Oil companies have been the first to take advantage of Saudi/OPEC efforts to raise oil prices, and the first to also demand retribution when OPEC has fought back by flooding the markets. I certainly don't condone the culture or repressive society of modern-day Saudi Arabia. However, in the energy sphere, where we are primarily concerned, Saudi Arabia has been far more of a victim of both U.S. government pressures and U.S. oil producers' behavior than an aggressor.

Now let's look at some other folks who we'd like to also turn into the kind of unwitting environmentalist that Saudi Arabia is progressively seeking to be,: U.S. oil companies.

CHAPTER 5:

OIL IS NOT THE ENEMY

O n March 10, 2019, Ethiopian Airlines flight 302 crashed within minutes of its takeoff, killing all of its 157 passengers. The plane being flown was a Boeing 737 MAX, which also was the plane in a very similar crash of a Lion Air flight in October 2018, where all 189 on that flight were also killed. Because of the similarities of these tragedies, an FAA order forced the grounding of all of Boeing's 393 737 MAX planes already in the air. Later investigations found a stabilizer on the plane was badly engineered during one update of the 737 class, with an almost certain negligence in the insufficient software fix that was applied by Boeing to these planes, now clearly understood to be the cause of both of the deadly crashes. Regulators have been slow and even reluctant to recognize suggested fixes by Boeing, and it is unclear when—or if—the 737 MAX might ever be returned to service, and whether the public will ever be re-assured enough to fly on the plane again.

Why do I tell this tragic story of airplanes in the middle of a book on oil?

Because there are lessons to be learned in the oil markets from it. In no way is the airline industry nearly as close to the center of the U.S. economy as oil and other fossil fuels are. But there is an interesting parallel to be noted from the 737 MAX incident and its subsequent effects on the economy at large. What is initially clear from the Boeing tragedy, besides the obvious loss of life, was the disaster that befell Boeing itself. Its CEO was forced to step down, and the production of the 737 has been suspended indefinitely. Its stock has also been pummeled—as you can see in Figure 5.1—during a moment when the stock market has continued to rally strongly. Previously, Boeing had been an integral part of our already 10-year-old stock rally.

Figure 5.1
S&P 500 Index vs. Boeing (BA)
March-December 2019

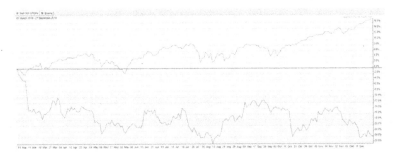

We may not care much about the concurrent tragedy that befell Boeing stock in light of the company's obvious engineering negligence. But the point is that Boeing was not the only victim of its mistakes. Several innocent industries and thousands of jobs have depended on the continued success of Boeing and specifically the continued production of the 737. The ripple effects of Boeing's troubles are being felt through hundreds of suppliers, both small and large.

From radar systems to seat fabric, aluminum tubing to specialty fasteners, the complexity of a single airplane from a major manufacturer being grounded has reverberated strongly through the entire U.S. economy. Safran, a supplier of engines for the MAX, along with U.S. powerhouse GE, depend almost completely on the plane's production. An $8b company in Kansas relies on the MAX for 80% of its work making fuselages. GE's own revenues have been reassessed downwards by $400m per quarter.

These larger suppliers, of course, rely on suppliers of their own—and the circle of the MAX's downfall expands ever wider: The current estimate is that 8,000 businesses will be impacted by the shutdown of production of the 737 MAX. While this shutdown costs Boeing itself an estimated $2b a month, the multiplier effect of lost economic activity from all of those suppliers is estimated to be perhaps as much as a hundred times that. High-paying jobs will be furloughed or even cut for thousands, and the loss of this one plane is estimated by Moody's to likely cut as much as two tenths of a percentage point off of U.S. GDP growth.

DREAMS VS. REALITY – AN HONEST TIMELINE FOR TRANSITIONING TO RENEWABLES

With the Boeing story in mind, let's talk about a truly possible, and truly practical, mechanism and timeline for the replacement of fossil fuels with renewable energy sources.

I am a big fan of Greta Thunberg, the 16-year old Swedish girl who has received international acclaim after her fervent, accusatory speech to the United Nations Climate Action Summit in 2019.

"How dare you?!" (Her most-quoted line.) "You have stolen my dreams and my childhood with your empty words. And yet I'm one of the lucky ones. People are suffering. People are dying. Entire ecosystems are collapsing. We are in the beginning of a mass extinction. And all you can talk about is money and fairy tales of eternal economic growth. How dare you!"

"You are failing us," Thunberg concluded. "But the young people are starting to understand your betrayal. The eyes of all future generations are on you. And if you choose to fail us, I say: We will never forgive you."

This speech has inspired school sit-ins for climate activism and earned Thunberg a *Time* magazine cover for Person of the Year and even a nomination for the Nobel Peace Prize (!). I have tremendous respect for this girl's activism and commitment, and I couldn't agree more with the goals that she is attempting to promote.

But Thunberg isn't an energy expert, she isn't a climate expert, and she's not an economist. As zealous as she (and countless others) obviously are about the effects of climate change, she couldn't possibly understand the concurrent negative impacts to the tens of millions of people from the changes in entrenched economic forces she's speaking of quickly reversing. I know, I know: what good are economic benefits in a world that is fast reaching the tipping point of ecological disaster? Believe me, I get it. But there is, even in the most primary question of the safety of the global environment, things that are possible and things that are not possible in the current world we live in. We can admire a young girl's passion, and we can appreciate how she's empowering young people around the world.

But a better nomination for a Nobel prize might be reserved for the scientists and engineering analysts who are charting the very complex, difficult, and possible paths to a more sustainable energy infrastructure. As real as the risks of climate change are, there remain other, more practical paths to a renewable future than scowling into a microphone and calling for the immediate end of all fossil-fuel production and use. I hope that this book might become a part of one of those paths.

One more example to get me in trouble with nearly everyone before I return to talking about energy markets: A recent study by Stanford professor Mark Jacobson (who is certainly qualified as an expert on climate) opined that the complete conversion from fossil fuels to renewables in the United States could pay for itself in 7 years. The study (a culmination of several the environmental engineering professor has undertaken since 2010) proposed that the building of the infrastructure to provide 100% sustainable energy to the U.S. for transport, manufacturing, lighting, and heating would cost $73 trillion, a truly unfathomable sum. Yet the study also maintains that this massive proposed conversion, through higher efficiency gains, would result in a savings of more than $11 trillion a year—hence, Jacobson's 7-year prediction for recouping the investment. "There's really no downside to making this transition," Jacobson said optimistically when releasing his report.

It doesn't make much difference whether the professor is right or wrong, either on his conversion costs or his estimates at efficiency savings—both of which, I imagine, are based on countless assumptions that are impossible to verify before the fact, or probably even after it. What is clear is that neither this study, nor Jacobson's work in general—although a fantastic academic exercise in the possibilities of a concerted national effort towards reimagining the national energy infrastructure—doesn't even begin to assess what effects that conversion might have on the U.S. economy and the people inside it, who are merely trying to live their lives.

In my first book, *Oil's Endless Bid,* I wrote about the incredible interconnectedness of fossil fuels with the U.S. economy. Although that book was written in 2011 and has seen fossil fuels weaken their grip on the economy quite a bit here in the U.S., it remains incredibly significant. We are not a completely oil-reliant nation like Saudi Arabia, whose oil revenues are more than 70% of the GDP, or Russia, where it is still a whopping 30%. Here in the U.S., fossil fuels account for less than 8% of our economy. It would seem then that the U.S. is ripe for just such a conversion, but just as in the story with Boeing's 737 MAX, the costs for displacing such a significant cog of the U.S. economy has a multiplier effect that goes well beyond the 8% of GDP that represents oil companies.

Fully 40% of companies that make up the S+P 500 are at least 50% engaged in energy prices to keep their business afloat. What I mean by that is that none of these businesses operate without a very deep interest in the costs and the type of energy that is available. There are many of these businesses you wouldn't ever consider as 'energy' companies, but for their bottom line, they might as well be.

For example, most raw materials companies of any kind are immensely reliant on energy, and not just those that procure fossil fuels. Aluminum production requires massive heat in smelting bauxite, and Alcoa (for example) has spent billions on securing some energy producers of their own, so they are not as likely to be derailed by spiking energy costs. Much the same goes for companies that take iron ore and turn it into steel, or take rubber and other fossil-fuel-based composites and turn it into tires, melt sand and turn it into glass, or any of the thousands of companies that take any raw material or combination of them and manufacture precision component parts. These costs then bleed strongly into manufacturing of all kinds, whether that's for automobiles or heavy machinery or airplanes, and the costs of energy will greatly affect their costs for these components and their bottom lines.

We could then consider all the companies in the United States that rely on transport: the entirety of shipping companies, FedEx, UPS, DHL, and (of course) Amazon. The airlines are notably sensitive to jet fuel price swings, and many engage in hedging in the futures markets to reduce their risk.

Then there's refrigeration and food services—all heavily reliant on energy to keep food fresh. And these are the ones that are most reliant on energy. Of course, there are many more examples of commerce that does not operate without an eye on energy prices, because so much of their costs are tied to them.

As we discuss all of these businesses that are either directly reliant on energy or indirectly so, there is another pattern that emerges. While the oil and gas industry in America takes credit for 9 million jobs, neither are these companies that are indirectly reliant on energy overwhelmingly fueled by low-cost labor either: Dow Chemical, American Airlines, Alcoa, Dunlop, Corning, and on and on—all of these companies are stocked with trained workers, mid-management employees, and highly paid executives, certainly many times the multiple of those employed by oil companies alone. These highly trained and highly paid workers are the single salaries that support millions of middle-class families, with five- and often six-figure paychecks. We're not talking about jobs in a Wal-Mart or a Starbucks when we talk about energy-reliant industries. Instead, when we talk about crippling the fossil fuels supply and the commerce that's associated with it, we must remember we're also talking about the disruption of millions of middle-class families, too.

Of course, no environmentalist really bothers much to think about the businesses that rely directly on fossil fuels like Exxon or Shell, preferring that most of these 'oil hogs' either retool or go out of business altogether. But, of course, it is not the businesses that we much care about either; it is the people who are employed, both directly and indirectly, by them and, moreover, by the interactive commerce that drives our country's economy that we must take into account. We cannot undertake any kind of rational, whole-scale change in the infrastructure that powers our economy without considering the effects on the millions of Americans who rely on that economy to live their lives.

In 2010, activist Josh Fox released the documentary *Gasland,* an examination of the growing environmental impacts of natural-gas fracking on the Marcellus shale region of Pennsylvania. One image from that film continued to resonate with environmentalists across the country for years, that of a local resident living on adjacently leased acreage lighting his sink tap on fire, flaring the aerated natural gas that was a part of his local water supply. This image of burning tap water came at a time when the possibilities of advancement for natural gas as the 'next step' in our energy evolutionary chain was near its apex. Looking back at that moment, the vast success that was being felt from natural-gas fracking was at its peak: prices were dropping, oil companies were seeing tremendous gains, and the "Pickens plan" of natural gas transport possibilities for cars and trucks was a seriously considered option of U.S. energy policy in Washington.

One image destroyed all of that. Environmentalists ready to latch onto any rationale to abandon fossil fuels in their entirety latched onto that image of burning water and replayed it over and over, causing a public panic and forcing legislatures into restrictions on natural gas that the industry didn't need while ignoring those restrictions that they did. In Washington, any advocacy of natural gas became an untouchable political issue, and the national move towards natural gas was stopped in its tracks.

In hindsight, that flaming tap was the victim of associated gas that had been part of the aquifer for centuries, where natural gas had been seeping out of the ground and into the water supply since the Cenozoic era and not much affected by the fracking that was going on next door. In fact, there have been tens of thousands of fracked natural-gas wells in the Marcellus and elsewhere across the country, with only the handful of cases that have been proven to have even minor leakage of gas into neighboring aquifers. In the interim since 2010, the technology has quickly provided for a full and easy cementing fix of those that did leak. Consequently, there have been few complaints of leaking gas into tap water since, because this technical challenge was easily solved.

In 2010, *Gasland* was a hit for Josh Fox, while the follow-up *Gasland 2* in 2013 was a bust, but the damage was already done. This is not to say that the fracking of natural gas doesn't have any environmental challenges; it has plenty, including methane leaking and purposeful venting and flaring, disposal of wastewater from fracking, and several others. What I'm saying is that the people best equipped to find and fix the problems as well as assess the benefits and risks of national energy policy are not likely to be the activist documentarians, nor 16-year-old impassioned young folks, nor (to be fair) energy company industry lobbyists and paid advocates.

One further example: Legal challenges from environmentalists on oil and gas pipelines have been a huge initiative since the landmark protests began against the building of the Keystone XL pipeline in 2010. The Keystone project was a proposed build-out of an already existing pipeline running from Hardesty, Canada into the United States, terminating in Northern Kansas. Its phase-4 expansion was designed to be a more modern and direct route for Alberta oil sands crude, but environmentalists opposed the increased transport of oil sands, the 'dirtiest' of crude grades, and the proposed route of the pipeline through the unspoiled lands of Montana, South Dakota, and Nebraska. Protests led by 350.org attracted national attention, including attendance by several celebrities, including Daryl Hannah and Mark Ruffalo.

The success of these demonstrations in slowing Keystone were proven when President Obama delayed the approval of the pipeline, in essence putting the questions of approval for all U.S. pipelines in the slow hands of the courts. Despite the push forward for the project by President Trump in 2017, the approval for Keystone XL is still in the hands of the courts, nearly 7 years later. In retrospect, the environmentalists did TransCanada (now TC Energy) a huge favor, as the huge gluts of U.S. domestic crude oil would have made further transport of Canadian oil sands a financial failure, but that's neither here nor there. What it more importantly did was give environmental groups a game plan for opposing all levels of oil and gas infrastructure: oppose every pipeline, no matter its purpose; force its approval process into the courts; push for delay after delay with the hope that the pipeline developer's patience and money would run out. This has been most destructive in the vast slowdown of pipeline buildouts for natural gas, where the lack of complete networks has kept basis differentials (the difference in prices) for natural gas huge in large metropolitan areas compared to average national prices, while greatly slowing the infrastructure needed to make the transition of natural gas from crude oil far easier and quicker.

Figure 5.2.
Natural Gas Pipelines Get Tougher to Build

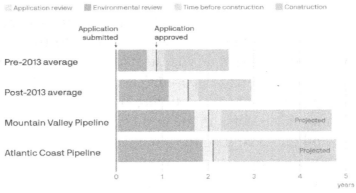

Reproduced from LawIQ; Chart: Axios Visuals

Since the 'success' of the Keystone XL protests, the average time needed for approvals for natural-gas pipelines has increased by more than a year as shown in Figure 5.2, and two of the most-needed pipelines—the Atlantic Coast pipeline (slated to run through Virginia to feed the East Coast markets in Virginia and North Carolina) and the Mountain Valley pipeline (also slated to service coastal Virginia)—are both mired in lawsuits that have been ongoing for more than 4 years. Both pipelines would bring additional natural gas supply that would help not only to offset current utility use of coal and heating oil, but would supplement the associated energy needs for rapidly growing solar and wind renewable energy projects.

To put a point on the ultimate waste of court resources being abused by environmental groups, the Supreme Court, in a 2020 decision, approved by 7-2 the U.S. Forestry decision to allow the 600-mile Atlantic Coast pipeline to be built under sections of the Appalachian Trail, and other major pipelines are expected to be ultimately approved as well. (An update: As of early July 2020, Duke Energy and Dominion Resources threw in the towel on the Atlantic Coast pipeline after its seven-year fight, abandoning the project altogether, despite their long-winded but successful rulings in court).

In short, there are pipeline projects that are environmental disasters, bringing unneeded and filthy oil into the United States with little financial upside, such as Keystone XL, which was fairly and correctly opposed. There are also far more needed and important infrastructure buildouts that will deliver cheaper natural gas that can displace dirtier and more expensive oil and coal, like the Atlantic Coast pipeline—and environmentalists can't or don't want to make any distinction between the two. Both the good and the bad are similarly and equally enthusiastically being opposed, merely because they are associated with fossil fuels, and that's all the information the environmental lobbies seem to need to know. The success of opposing projects that are actually good—the ones that are pushing forward the transitions to natural gas and therefore renewables from dirty oil grades and coal—are heralded as equally important, when they are in fact restraining the transition to cleaner and ultimately more sustainable sources.

Most important, I want to try to make the point that oil (and gas) are not really the universal enemy here. While the current trend in politics and the media is to ignore the connections between fossil fuels and the rest of the U.S. economy and its integration into our daily lives, they are, in fact, at the focal center, bound up together. And while we can strive to change the relationships that have grown between fossil fuels and the economy that has been powered by it for more than 100 years, we must recognize the massive dislocations that will take place if we move too quickly away from them, and particularly without a well-considered plan.

CAN WE GET OIL COMPANIES TO LOVE RENEWABLES?

Oil companies are no fools.

Let me revise that.

Although oil companies have made tremendous mistakes in their pursuit of profits, they are no less aware of the inevitable march towards renewable energy as you or I. In fact, it should seem quite obvious that their superior perspective on the development of energy sources and uses gives them a far better insight into the likely speed and inevitability of sustainable energy. Yes, they have a vested interest in pushing that inevitability as far into the future as they can, but there is ample evidence that they not only accept the coming of this change, but they have spent billions of dollars in preparing for it, and that they will be ready for it. Long before the drumbeat of Climate Change got to the level to inspire the Paris Climate accords, oil companies had been spending billions on developing alternative energy sources.

For Exxon, it must be admitted that most of its efforts still concentrated on fossil fuels as the end result, with both the conversion of natural gas to gasoline and Exxon's particular concentration on algae-based biofuels – but it is now an outlier among the big majors. BP, for example, famously put a not-insignificant $10 billion dollars into developing alternative energy in the 1990s, during its somewhat strange "beyond petroleum" campaign. Although much cynicism was heaped on this effort, with many calling it an expensive PR campaign of "Greenwashing," with little real interest in solar and wind. But to its credit, BP certainly put a mountain of cash behind the effort—and suffered fairly horrible monetary losses from it. One would be very cynical indeed to think that the entirety of the effort was merely an expensive, yet phony, curtain dressing. Today, BP has again returned as a leader to the sustainable energy sector, setting a 'carbon-zero' goal of completely carbon-free energy production by 2050. Shell might be the most committed for the longest time to alternative energy, including long-standing divisions created inside the company to develop both solar and wind power. No matter where these multinationals devoted time and energy into alternative sources, there was one clear pattern, however: the early efforts of mega-cap international oil companies on sustainable energy development has been consistently met with financial failure.

Why was this? One reason is that the United States government has signaled inconsistently, moving in one direction for one administration, and then backpedaling in the other during the next. In fact, for nearly 50 years, the U.S. has struggled

to find a consistent energy policy and timeline for its movement away from oil and towards natural gas and ultimately
sustainable energy sources. Without an agreed-on long-term
energy plan, incentives and regulatory focus has ping-ponged
back and forth between conservative Republican administrations who weren't interested in committing long-term federal
funding to support development of renewable energy and
Democratic administrations who were more committed to
funding, but still were restrained by the budgetary concerns
both on Capitol hill and with voters in politically important
'oil states.' Subsidies (when they were in place) were never
given much forward life, and were in constant need of Congressional and White House renewal, and who and what party
occupied the White House had everything to do with whether
those incentives would be continued.

Such inability to plan confidently on forward costs caused
both frustration from those multinationals willing to invest in
alternatives; even more than frustration, it caused billions of
dollars of write-downs of alternative energy investment. Projects that were cost-contained during one administration using government incentives and tax rebates would find their
costs spiraling out of control when they were removed in the
next one.

It wasn't until President Obama created reliable funding for
solar projects that U.S. solar companies could enter the capital markets as true global competitors for this growing energy
sector. But one need only remember the fallout from the false
Solyndra narrative to see what this initiative cost Democrats
in political capital in fossil-fuel rich states. And while solar
subsidies remain at least marginally on the books today, the
Trump administration has (not surprisingly) worked hard to
reverse these budget outlays, as well as remove regulatory
roadblocks for further fossil-fuel investment at the expense of
renewables. With another reversal in government support,

(and low fossil fuel prices to compete with), investment of the United States overall into renewables took its first downturn in 2019 in the previous three years.

A second reason (which is important for the thesis of this book) is that oil prices have not maintained triple-digit prices long enough for much of that new technology to take hold. Throughout this book, I've talked specifically about the price of oil and what it has meant for alternative energy markets and initiatives. As hard as it is to believe now, most oil analysts—and oil companies in general—had relied on an oil price that since 2005 had hovered near $100 a barrel and even above (removing the anomaly of the 2008-2009 economic crisis). They expected oil prices to remain elevated, literally forever. Instead, because prices frequently were depressed, their investments in sustainable energy never reached a point where they were even closely competitive in the open market compared to the fossil fuels they were already selling. While a few of the oil companies have continued their investments into renewable energy, most had abandoned any significant outlays into those technologies years ago.

But all that seems to be changing, again, and rapidly. The interest and newfound awareness in climate change has had a mostly unnoticed but very significant effect on major oil companies, admittedly more in European majors than in the United States, but with U.S. majors not far behind.

Of course, the incredible work of activists and the collective effort of the Paris Climate accords has had much to do with this. But pressure has been coming from other sources besides the traditional sources like Greenpeace and Bill McKibben's 360.org. It seems that environmental activism has had at least as important an effect on raising awareness of investors as on the oil companies themselves. Consequently, collectivized efforts by shareholders of oil companies have demanded more accountability for climate change, and public class-action lawsuits have forced the management of these companies to respond.

The most important of these suits has been the fraud case brought against Exxon Mobil by the State Attorney General in New York. In it, the State plaintiff claimed that Exxon was well aware of the effects of fossil fuels on the climate even during the 1980s and engaged in a long campaign of fraud to cover up those environmental costs. Subpoenaed documents from Exxon scientists have confirmed that they were as up to date as environmental advocates have been and documented to senior management the possible ill effects of burning fossil fuels on the air and water. Even with these damning documents at their disposal, the State Attorney General lost its case to Exxon in late 2019, ending a five-year effort starting in 2015. Still, the effort to hold the largest U.S. oil company accountable for fossil-fuel emissions has helped add pressure for change elsewhere in the industry.

The first most notable and important breakthrough has been the oil companies' public support of carbon taxes—a 360-degree turnaround from their positions even five years ago. In May of 2019, executives from four majors—Exxon, BP, Shell, and ConocoPhillips—joined with the larger Climate Leadership Council, a group representing more than 75 Fortune 500 companies, and they traveled to Washington to testify at Congressional hearings and put their support behind a carbon tax. I believe carbon taxes are an absolutely necessary step in pushing markets towards natural gas and renewables and have proven themselves useful in Europe already. Several Democratic attempts at creating a "carbon market" here in the U.S. have fallen flat with the GOP and subsequently never gained much traction in the past. However, with many of the largest U.S. oil companies now willing to consider them and include them in their long-term capital expenditure and development plans, it certainly looks like it's long past time to reestablish the initiative again, no matter who controls Congress. It is astoundingly significant that even those oil companies that were noted as historically unmovable climate-change 'deniers' like Exxon have publicly advocated for carbon taxes in the last few years.

Besides carbon tax advocacy with the Climate Leadership Council, other oil companies have joined with other, even more aggressive renewable-friendly organizations. Total, the French energy giant, has signed on as a partner in the Breakthrough Energy coalition, comprising mostly hedge fund managers and other wealthy corporate philanthropists, such as Bill Gates, Michael Bloomberg, and Jeff Bezos. The list of high-powered fund managers reads as a *Who's Who* of the most successful and deeply capitalized players in the business, including Ray Dalio of Bridgewater Capital, Julian Robertson of Tiger funds, and George Soros. But the Breakthrough Energy Coalition isn't seeking to use its well-heeled influence to get governments to move and change their policy thinking towards climate change; it is directly funding research and development of alternative technologies themselves, with their own collectively sourced funding.

That a major oil company is committed as well to be a part of this effort that, supposedly, is at competitive odds with their own is a telling indication of how oil companies are changing their views towards climate change and how to manage their own businesses in the future. Shell has probably been the most aggressive of all the majors in investing its own money to developing alternative energy, spending about $2 billion a year in 2018, far more than any other major oil company. But it has taken an even stronger symbolic step by withdrawing itself from the American Fuel and Petrochemical Manufacturers Association in 2020, leaving a trade group that along with the American Petroleum Institute has been the most resistant to climate-change science and the firmest supporters of the fossil fuels industry for decades. In choosing to leave, Shell specifically cited the disconnect with the stance of the AFPM towards climate change. It is the first oil company to leave an oil advocacy trade association that virtually every other oil major is a member of and supports.

Although Shell is perhaps alone in its disassociation from a major oil trade group, it is hardly alone in its significant investments in renewable energy. Total has announced that it intends to have 20% of its energy supply represented by renewables by 2035. BP has also reinitiated green energy efforts within the company, building on the remnants of its 'beyond petroleum' campaign. In addition to those remaining assets in wind farms and biofuels, BP has recently invested $200m in a European solar company, Lightsource, and has allocated about $500m more to lower carbon technologies in 2018. It's still a small part of BP's $16b total budget, but it represents a significant increase for them. Statoil, the Norwegian oil major, is hoping to reinvent itself as a balanced energy company in light of declining production from its major North Sea oil assets. It has invested more than $2b into North Sea wind farms and promises to have 20% of its energy supply in sustainable technologies by 2030.

The idea that all of these efforts from so many of the most powerful members of the oil and gas industry are mere 'greenwashing' is absurd. Instead, it is clear that major oil companies are painfully aware of the trends away from fossil fuels and are making their best efforts to be a part of them.

And that's the point – WE HAVE TO LET THEM.

Read

LIKE IT OR NOT, OIL'S HERE TO STAY

I wake up in the cold on a January morning: the heat seems to have gone off overnight. I scramble out of bed and check the thermostat and then the boiler. It seems a valve has tripped, stopping the flow of the natural gas from the underground lines supplying everyone on my block. I call my local gas company, but it has already sent me a text message, advising me of the problem and that service had already been restored. I reset my boiler in the basement and relight the pilot, and I hear the hum as it trips on and begins to reheat my house.

I go upstairs and power on my coffee maker, the electricity from the local power company flowing seamlessly through the lines outside my house into the outlets. More gas powers the hot water heater that gives me my hot shower that energizes me to start my day. As I slip into my car on the way to my office, I notice I'm low on gas and slide through the local BP station to refuel. My car is a modern one, full of precision steel, aluminum, and plastic parts, all of which required major inputs of fossil fuels or the energy from them to be manufactured.

Here it is, barely 9AM on a typical morning, and I've already had dozens of important interactions with the oil and gas world, whether I wanted to or not. We're all reliant in our modern lives on the work that the oil and gas industries do, and it would be impossible to imagine modern life without them.

I'm not trying to make a public relations presentation for the sake of oil companies. Instead, I want to try and establish how deeply involved our lives already are with energy companies and make another point: Try to imagine how quickly we could transition towards a sustainable, energy-efficient world if we somehow could bring this vast knowledge and interconnectedness of U.S. and international energy companies to bear on this critical problem of our time.

What if we could make energy companies WANT to move towards solar and wind energy, or at least be advocates for them becoming a more significant share of the energy pie? It is very clear that no one understands the costs, benefits, and risks better, and no one has any better understanding of the transport, distribution, and infrastructure requirements. Heck, no one has more CONTROL of all of the systems we'd need to fully integrate solar, wind, and other renewable sources of energy into our grid of existing fossil fuel and electricity supplies. The question isn't whether the oil companies are the best equipped to take us to a clean renewable energy future, they are the only ones who are equipped. Instead, the question is why isn't using the energy companies in our bold new world vision of sustainable energy not even considered an option in the discussions (or, at least, any of the discussions I hear) on climate change and renewables?

The answer seems obvious to almost everyone: it's because clean carbon energy production is at odds with the business model of fossil fuel producers. Everyone has seemed to take this as an obvious, incontrovertible fact. Only I think that the first part of the chapter I've written has made a case that, perhaps, this is not so obvious as it might seem anymore.

Before I lay out the possibilities of using the oil companies as our main, market-based road towards renewables, let's consider the alternative—the one that has dominated environmental arguments from the left and has been growing in volume as the climate change debate has intensified in recent years: that oil (and the oil companies) are the enemy. I can understand this argument very well, and I might even have agreed with it several years ago. Exxon Mobil, during the time of CEO Lee Raymond, was famously a denier of climate change and paid anti-environmental groups millions of dollars to campaign against the growing mountain of environmental science connecting the burning of carbon to temperature rises and extreme weather. Most of the majors lined up behind Exxon in their support of petroleum advocacy and lobbying groups to deter environmental regulation restricting fossil fuels.

We've only very, very recently seen the majors progress towards admitting the truth of climate science. But even without the break that Shell and others have begun to make away from the idea of a complete monopoly of fossil fuels in the energy supply chain, the last 20 years of fighting with the oil companies to secure a sustainable path towards lowered carbon emissions has been, in a word, fruitless.

And it's no wonder. During the winter of 2020, I watched one of the many Democratic debates for President. Two of the candidates on stage, Bernie Sanders and Elizabeth Warren, had planks in their platforms looking to federally outlaw fracking—all fracking, no matter where or how it is being operated. This is nothing new for the left wing of the Democratic party, and it has been a long-term goal of many on the left for years. For oil companies, this threat to the new and transformative technologies of shale oil and natural gas that have revitalized U.S. oil exploration and production has been met with all the resistance and political influence they can muster.

As I've pointed out, oil companies are so deeply connected to the health of the economy and to our modern lives that they have almost unlimited resources to fight against proposals like this that look to limit their market potential or even possibly put them out of business. It's not just with paid lobbyists that they ply their influence. Oil-rich states in Texas, Arkansas, North Dakota, Nebraska, Alaska, California, New Mexico, Pennsylvania, and others employ millions of people in the oil and gas business in well-paying jobs, and those folks send Congressmen and Senators to Washington that are necessarily oil and gas advocates themselves. Exxon we know, has spent millions empowering anti-climate science reports from paid institutions to enter into the public record for more than a decade. Most of the energy companies have been members of trade organizations, like the American Petroleum Institute and the Natural Gas Council, which has spent tens of millions of public relations dollars on television and magazine advertisements extolling the virtues of fossil fuels.

In terms of the resources that are being brought to this particular fight, the environmental folks are vastly outgunned. Figures 5.3 and 5.4 are taken from the website opensecrets.org, showing the totals oil and gas companies have given to influence the U.S. government, whether to lobbyist groups, shown in Figure 5.3, or to individual candidates and issue-organized party political action committees, shown in Figure 5.4. In 2016 alone, you're looking at a combined investment of nearly a quarter of a billion dollars from oil companies. That's some serious coin.

Figure 5.3.
Money Spent Annually on Lobbying for Oil & Gas, 1998-2019

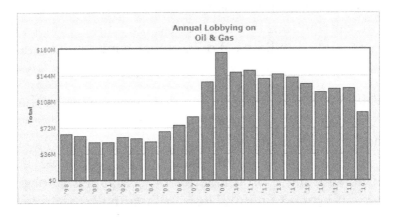

Figure 5.4.
Dollars Spent by Oil & Gas on Political Campaigns

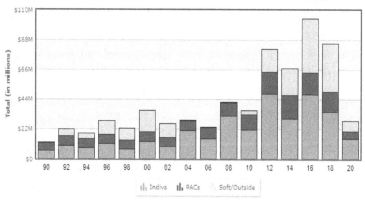

It's more than beyond the scope of this book to try and find a solution to the rampant flood of corporate money in U.S. politics and Capitol Hill lobbying. We can't attempt here to find a simple fix to the very complex and difficult problem of soft money in politics. My point instead is that it has been—and will continue to be—a difficult road to try and label and battle oil producers using money in Washington as the enemy to be destroyed. Their resources are unlimited, at least in comparison to what environmental groups can bring to the fight. We'll do a whole lot better if we can somehow create a collective plan that includes oil companies, that takes into account their critical contributions to our economy, the millions of jobs they promote, and the billions of dollars they contribute to the national GDP.

What if—instead of seeing oil and oil companies as the enemy—we could actually incentivize oil companies to integrate cleaner natural gas and ultimately carbon-zero energy sources, such as wind and solar, into their supply portfolios? If you could make it more profitable for oil companies to begin to develop and support natural gas and solar power than to continue searching and drilling for oil, they'd most certainly do it. In fact, it seems clear that even the most anti-environmental oil companies out there, including Exxon, have been making strides to prepare for this for years.

I'll give tremendous credit to the environmental folks over the last decade for doing the hard work of informing the public of the coming and truly dystopian effects of extreme weather and climate change. In this regard, we must even give a nod of appreciation to those celebrities, including Mark Ruffalo, Emma Thompson, and Robert Redford, and even Greta Thunberg for pushing the conversation forwards. But the time has come for us to find a purposeful policy that doesn't look to demonize the oil companies and the work they do and instead brings them inside the tent to help us enact the huge upstream and downstream changes that we'll need to make it all work. The oil companies are not only the best equipped to do this, they're the best able to do it as well. We'll need an integrated, long-term energy plan from Washington, one that the environmentalists are satisfied with and one that the oil companies can rely on as unshakable, no matter which party holds power. I'll make some suggestions towards these very big goals in Chapter 11.

But first, before anything, we have to figure out a way to break down the wall that is preventing both sides from getting to that negotiating table together. It is clear to me, having been a witness to this for the past 25 years, that the campaigns of divestiture and Greenpeace harassment of drill ships and drilling rigs and anti-fracking protests have not slowed down the oil and gas industry one little bit. The only thing that will truly turn their efforts towards renewables and away from fossil fuels is profits—and this is the incentive that must be employed to move our country, and our planet, forwards now. We rely on fossil fuels more than we want to admit, and the fact is that we'll need them, in large quantities, even if all the goals of sustainable energy development and use are universally agreed to tomorrow. If we really want to reach those goals, we're going to need energy companies pursuing them with as much vigor as environmentalists do. And we can make it worth their while to do so.

We've got oil companies, given the right conditions, ready to be partners in the transition towards renewables. I've maintained that the first, most important condition they'll need is a sustainably high price for oil. However, since the 2014 price bust and for several years leading up to it, it has been the botched opportunity of U.S. shale that has singularly prevented global prices from staying high. In the next chapter, we'll examine how that happened.

CHAPTER 6:

SHALE BOOM, SHALE BUST

I n 2015, I wrote a book entirely focused on the transformation of the U.S. oil industry by shale entitled *Shale Boom, Shale Bust,* but the intervening years have made clear just how prophetic that title has turned out to be. In no way was I expecting to see the full-scale greed, stupidity, and self-destructive behavior of independent oil companies that I have witnessed since I wrote that book, which only looked to make some opportunistic predictions on how investors might benefit from the explosion of oil coming from shale, in light of the price collapse of 2014.

In retrospect, I believe it's now become vital to examine what happened in those five years of unbelievable growth since and what is happening now in the procurement of oil from shale here in the United States. What I've seen over those years is an industry that has frankly run amok, wasting our national resources unnecessarily, putting our environment at risk, and flushing tens of billions of investor dollars down the drain when alternatively tens of billions of dollars should have been made instead. The U.S. shale industry has single-handedly destroyed the possibility of many millions of stable, long-term high-paying jobs and the opportunity to make the United States truly 'energy independent'—or at least as independent as America could be.

But most disappointing has been how shale oil has not merely flowed here in the U.S. in a disciplined way, but instead been forcibly hemorrhaged from our most precious natural stockpiles, unrestricted by either capital constraints or regulatory ones. Because of this, our environment has been perhaps irretrievably compromised where it didn't need to be.

Further, that unrelenting flood of oil has caused a systemic glut that has kept oil prices low for more than half a decade and counting. This has sapped companies of deserved profits and the United States of economic growth, and it has stifled innovation and capital flow to necessary renewable technologies. It is not too much to say that the U.S. shale industry has singularly sidetracked the entire planet in its inevitable march towards solar and wind—and perhaps doomed us all to a much more difficult future by the wasted time it has caused.

That's a lot of guilt to put on one lone energy sub-sector, I know. But let's take a look at how I come to these startling conclusions, and more important, how we can start to put it right.

FRACKING WILDCATTERS

From the start, fracking has been an exploit of excess. You need only look at the men who were at the forefront of the effort, their goals and their personal lives, to see it. I'm not trying to make poetry of the fracking revolution in the United States, but only one look at the lives of these pioneers of shale really puts the 'wild' in the old oil sobriquet of 'wildcatter.' Part of the fault for the excesses of shale oil need to be connected to the 'Wild West' romance towards these independent, entrepreneurial men. They spur the best images of our American free capitalist system, using their talent and hard work to seemingly rise 'from nothing' to attain great wealth. Their bold, confident 'American' visions of a new energy future inspired adulation and, from the Wall Street crowd, a readiness to invest. Let's look briefly at three of the biggest fracking 'heroes' to emerge from this time.

Hardly an oilman by trade, Aubrey McClendon came to the oil patch after a traditional ivy league education at Duke University. He returned to his home of Oklahoma City and founded Chesapeake energy with partner Tom Ward in 1982, drilling their first well in 1989. Newfound technologies of fracking for natural gas put McClendon and Chesapeake in hyperdrive, however. In the history of shale, no one can claim the title of confidence and conviction quite like Aubrey did at Chesapeake. Using his salesman's skills to accumulate capital and leverage up that investment to accumulate more and more leased acreage, McClendon ultimately controlled holdings for drilling shale wells larger than the size of the entire state of West Virginia.

But Aubrey's belief in shale didn't limit itself to the company he was running. During his time at the helm of Chesapeake, McClendon took most of his own compensation not in cash or stock but in personal ownership of leased acreage, keeping the public company more and more connected to his own personal success. And with acreage, McClendon knew no limits, both for the company and himself. He leveraged his own holdings using credit extended by the company itself, an impossible conflict in a publicly owned oil company.

But McClendon's wit, charm, and brash lifestyle kept his image as an American success story, one to be admired and trusted alive. He was generous with his time and money for several charitable causes in Chesapeake's hometown of Oklahoma City. And McClendon was a cool billionaire as well, the envy of many. He was a connoisseur of fine wines and fast sports cars and even bought a basketball team to bring to his hometown (the Thunder). While he was owner and CEO of

Chesapeake, he was a regular at OKC Thunder games, relishing his time courtside and often sharing his seats with his wife's cousin, supermodel Kate Upton. At his peak, Aubrey McClendon was certainly the most picture-perfect image of American success the energy world had ever seen.

But all came crashing down on him less than 5 years after that. With the oil markets swooning and McClendon's personal wealth exhausted, Aubrey's storybook life was cut short as his Chevy Tahoe slammed into an overpass embankment at 78 miles an hour, a week after the Justice department had revealed an indictment for lease contract price fixing—an indictment that few would say he did not deserve.

Without an ivy league education and with a history of dirty fingernails in the oil patch, Harold Hamm represented a more traditional 'wildcatter' than Aubrey McClendon. But Hamm was no less successful, turning the Bakken shale play of South Dakota into a reincarnation of the California gold rush and making Continental Resources into one of the largest independent exploration and production companies, worth nearly $30 billion at its height. Hamm worked his way up from nothing, truly staking everything on the shale prospects in the unknown Bakken shale play. Married twice, Hamm has had his own whirlwind personal life, committing multi-millions to Republican politics, and having the largest legal settlement in a divorce case on record at a near $1 billion.

Mark Papa turned what was once thought to be empty, used-up oil acreage into the fastest-growing shale play in the world in the Eagle Ford and again in the Permian of West Texas, making EOG Resources the premiere independent fracker in the United States and a consistent favorite of shale investors. Papa took EOG shares from $15 in 2004 to well over $100 in only 10 years, before retiring from the company with his victory arms raised, declaring that the 'shale boom was over' and that all the good money had already been made.

As dynamic as all these gentlemen were, it was hardly their swashbuckling confidence and hero-worship that propelled them to such great heights. The entire country was gripped in the 'mania' of shale fracking, taking all of Washington and the capital markets with it. It is only with 15 years of hindsight, after a decade and a half of intense U.S. fracking of oil and natural gas, that we can now assess these men and the real enterprise value of the businesses they started. In all cases, to quote Alan Greenspan on another market, 'irrational exuberance' ruled the industry during the earliest years of growth and continue to hound it to the present day.

This chapter includes a more exhaustive study of the trajectory of U.S. shale oil and how it happened, but the end results of the investments and investors into these three men and their companies tells a fairly complete story in itself, and it's not a good one: McClendon was forced to leave Chesapeake in disgrace as that company became embroiled in claims of shareholder fraud and rampant ill-advised credit extensions both for Chesapeake as a company and for McClendon personally at its head. Those shares continue to suffer from the outsized leverage it used at its peak, and shares have plummeted from a height of over $60 a share in 2008 to be currently measured in cents and fighting bankruptcy today. (Update: On June 28, 2020, Chesapeake filed for Chapter 11 protection). On his dismissal, McClendon immediately founded another fracking company, American Energy Partners, and promptly lost $5b of fresh capital there as well. McClendon remained an unbreakable advocate for fracking, even though the capital markets punished him in his later years consistently for his optimism.

Harold Hamm's Continental Resources is now a third of the size it was at its height, and although it remains one of the largest independent E&Ps in the U.S. and one of the remaining leaders in a Bakken shale play, every study on the remaining acreage in the Bakken shows that its best days are already behind them and the company's fortunes will, in all likelihood, continue to decline.

Mark Papa, after leaving a thriving EOG, decided not to take his own advice and also attempted to repeat his magic, accumulating nearly a half billion dollars in new capital in a special-purpose acquisition company (SPAC) called Silver Run Acquisitions. Ultimately, that fund was consolidated with the Permian specialist Centennial Resources. At the time of the merger, Centennial shares hovered near $20, but even the brilliance of Mark Papa couldn't change the coming bust in shale oil fracking. As of this writing in the early months of 2020, they are trading under $4, obviously in deep financial trouble. (Update: as of July 2020, Centennial Resources is trading under $1.)

All this to say that while these men (and several others) represented the best of the romantic vision of American capitalist bravado that has inspired U.S. innovation throughout history, something else was also clearly driving their earlier successes while just as quickly stopping them from repeating that magic in more recent years.

And that, of course, was money – and a lot of it.

THE GOLDEN ERA OF FRACKING, 2009-2014

To understand where that money was coming from and why it was coming in such unprecedented amounts, one has to first remember where the oil industry and the U.S. economy was during the 'golden era' of fracturing oil and gas from shale, between 2009-2014. On the back of a devastating economic collapse in 2008, capital markets had been repaired using enormous liquidity—i.e., credit—supplied by the U.S.

Treasury (and U.S. taxpayers). While the banking industry used this credit to repair the banks' own decimated balance sheets, they were also 'charged' with taking that excess liquidity and using it to stimulate the U.S. economy as well. And, while real estate proved to be a difficult place to reinvest (having been the sector that had driven the collapse in the first place), banks and other private funds were eager to find alternatives—any alternatives—that could be classified as 'safe' in which to create commerce in a recovering U.S. economy. Any alternative that could get the blessing of regulators and the Treasury, could create an opportunity to make back some of the vast capital the banks had lost in the financial crisis.

The newly developing technologies for first fracking natural gas wells proved just the ticket. The first commercially successful fracked natural gas well (using a modern mixture of sand, water, and chemicals) had just been conquered by Nick Steinsberger of Mitchell Energy in 2008. It created a revolution that quickly transformed the oil and gas industry in the United States.

The timing couldn't have been more propitious. During the years 2010-2012, the new techniques of 'slick-water' fracking were extended from shale gas to shale oil, which began to overtake the fracking of natural gas as a technology yielding unheard of new sources of energy, at a profit point far exceeding what a company could make from natural gas yields. Imagine the excitement from both Wall Street and the oil and gas industry to have a new, domestic, and cheap-looking source of natural gas and oil, just at a time when borrowing money was about as cheap as it had ever been and the U.S. capital markets were begging to practically give it away.

And give it away they did. Oil companies that had already been engaged for decades in more traditional exploration and production of conventional oil flocked to the new technology, using both the acreage they already leased in the Barnett, Eagle

Ford, Bakken, and Permian shale plays to access fracked oil, as well as accessing the capital markets that were falling over each other to lend them money to buy up other acreage for lease whose potential for fracked oil seemed limitless.

It's hard to know just how much capital was thrown at start-up E&Ps as well as established oil companies expanding into shale at this time, both through issuance of private credit, public market bonds, and stock investment. From private equity, there was an estimated $200b alone that was earmarked for investment in shale, but that clearly was just the very tip of the iceberg. Even taking the three companies I talked about earlier in this chapter (Continental Resources, EOG Resources, and Chesapeake Energy), the capital accumulation was stunning: at the start of 2003, Chesapeake had a market cap of around $8b, but at its height in 2008 before the financial collapse, its worth was nearer to $100 billion. For EOG Resources, the growth in the same time period was from $6b to around $40b. But Harold Hamm's fortunes increased most stunningly: His company, Continental Resources, had only debuted in May 2007 at $7.45 a share with a market cap of $2.75 billion. In a little more than a year before the onset of the financial crisis, Hamm saw his company increase in value more than fourfold, to nearly $13 billion.

And the financial crisis, as I have noted, was only an accelerant to the mania that fracking had become. It was after the crisis that even more money spilled into the independent exploration and production energy companies in the United States. Hamm's $13 billion company on the eve of the 2008 financial crisis finally topped out to a value of nearly $30 billion before the second collapse of the energy markets in 2014. I outline each of the very important "three phases" of the 2014 oil bust in Chapter 9.

I've spoken only about three medium-sized American E&Ps to demonstrate just how much money and interest was being heaped on frackers. But it can't be forgotten how many hundreds of small oil companies were started with small lease holdings or pivoted away from more traditional oil production to get a piece of the hot Bakken, Eagle Ford, and Permian shale plays, as well as a dozen other plays whose potential seemed to be as good if not better than these three. Who knows how much capital was ultimately loaned and directly invested in U.S. shale? Certainly, the number must be in the several trillions of dollars, a number usually reserved for marking the gross national product of several independent European and emerging market nations.

That's a lot of money.

And what did the oil companies do with all of that money? Well, they fracked wells, of course. A lot of wells.

Figure 6.1.
The U.S. Shale "Gold Rush"

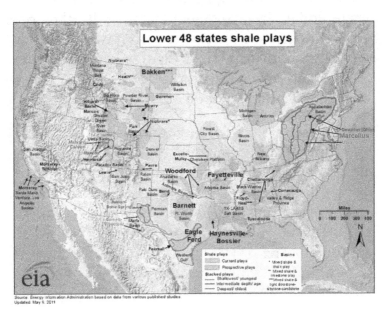

However, just like with the California gold rush of the 1850s, not every 'claim' turned out to contain the 'mother lode.' Fracking was a new technology, and the limits of it were not yet known. Neither was the new science of shale geology for drilling—finding quality shale formations that would yield good results—well-established, either. Plenty of the many shale plays (shown in Figure 6.1) that seemed to have the possibility of great returns in oil and gas turned out to be busts, or partial ones: the Barnett, Antrim of Michigan, The Monterey in California, the Mississippi Lime (and, to a lesser degree, the Haynesville, Uinta of Utah, and the Woodford-Cana) all proved to be less than efficient, or downright unsuitable for fracking.

Despite these risky initial investments in shale all over the United States, the mania to find, drill, and produce fracked oil and gas at that time made it very, very easy to find capital for start-ups and, in some cases, well-established oil companies in these emerging shale plays. These plays took billions of dollars in investment capital, with the hopes of every other oil investment since the first well from the first wildcatter at Spindletop was drilled—a gusher, the mother lode, an oil gold rush—and an oversized return on that investment that would go with it.

However, over time, and after countless billions of dollars of exploratory drilling, most of these plays showed more complex geology than was originally hoped, making fracking more difficult, more expensive, or both. Those who sank money into these areas were destined to experience negative returns when oil prices turned down anywhere below $100 a barrel or when natural gas prices turned under $4 per mmBtu, which they did with amazing speed after 2014.

Most of the companies that concentrated in these areas are mere memories now, having either gone bankrupt or become hollowed-out holding companies, having been forced to sell off any remaining assets of value to make some amends to the investors who sponsored them. For the most part, much of the hundreds of billions of dollars invested there is gone, never to return.

And what about the companies engaged in the most efficient and productive shale plays in America: the ones that have gotten all the press, and most of the money since 2010, specifically in the Bakken of South Dakota, the Eagle Ford in West Texas, and more recently in the Permian basin, extending through the west of Texas and into New Mexico? My book *Shale Boom, Shale Bust* concentrated on these areas and the companies that were working them in 2015. In Chapter 2 of that book, I spent a lot of time discussing the self-destructive cycle of drilling and capital burn that virtually every American E&P had fallen into in these 'hot' shale plays, in one form or another, since 2011, and even more self-destructively during the downturn of oil prices since 2014. In many ways, the trajectory of many of these companies are playing out now in precisely the same way as the more adventurous ones in the less economic plays that have been largely abandoned since 2014, with the only difference that they are doing it more slowly. That chapter was entitled "Shale is a Ponzi Scheme," and it's worth laying out the reasons for that provocative title of the self-destructive pattern in shale oil production (though in less detail here).

The production profile of shale oil wells is important to understand because it's not like any other oil wells that the oil industry has encountered in the past. When you drill a 'traditional' well, whether that be on land or offshore, that well tends to give you a fairly steady volume return of oil for many years before starting to tail off, as the natural pressure decreases and it empties. Not so with shale oil wells. They instead have a very high return rate when they are initially tapped, and they tend to fall off very quickly, usually within 6-18 months. After that, the volumes become inconsequential and are often abandoned or even sold to "stripper" well companies, the small-barrel-specialist vultures of the oil world.

Figure 6.2 is a chart from my friend Enno Peters from his great service Shaleprofile.com. It shows the production profile of all shale wells in the U.S. from 2010 onwards in their first year of service. It represents perfectly how shale wells are entirely different from other, more traditional wells. You can see how the production peaks quickly and declines just as quickly. In the early years of manic oil fracking (2010 through 2012), fracked wells would deliver more than 90% of their peak volumes after only 12 months after being tapped. Even taking into account the current, admittedly tremendous technological advances in shale production shown in the chart for later years, volumes currently still show more than 70% of a typical well's total volume will be gone after only one year of pumping.

Figure 6.2.
Fast Peaking of U.S. Shale Oil Well Volumes

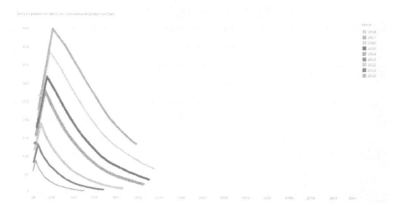

And from there, the erosion of production volume of shale wells only accelerates, as you can see in Figures 6.3 and 6.4:

Figure 6.3.
Daily Shale Oil Well Production (Years in Production)
Figure 6.4.
Annual Decline Rate (Years in Production)

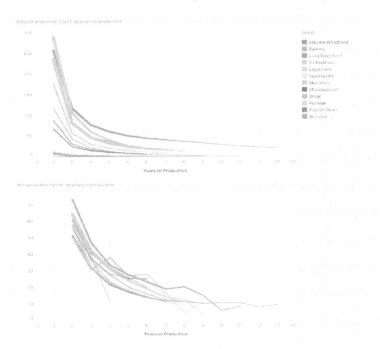

You can see that even by Year 2, most shale wells in every U.S. productive shale play are delivering a fraction of the volumes they did in their first year, and by Year 4, most are dripping only a few barrels a day for their operators and have become virtually useless.

This makes shale a very, very different business from 'traditional' oil production. It's also a very, very different investment for both shareholders and banks delivering credit. And that's when the industry begins to get into trouble.

THE TREADMILL BUSINESS OF A TYPICAL SHALE PRODUCER

Let's take an average shale producer starting up in the year 2011—a great year to be a fracker—and see what his business might look like.

Let's imagine a start-up shale oil company. Our company—let's call it ABC Oil—has no capital of its own, and for the sake of our model, ABC needs to borrow every dime it can to get it up and running producing oil. We've already established that's not a problem, because financing for even marginally good acreage was feverishly chasing high ($100+) oil prices in the years from 2010-2014. Let's even say that ABC has managed to find and sign leases for acreage on or near other prime acreage that has been delivering solid drilling results for other, bigger oil companies. This makes it even easier for ABC to find financing at 'regular' high-yield bond rates of 5-7%. Comparatively low rates like this for very risky B- to CCC-rated paper was one of the main reasons for the whirlwind development of shale production at the start of the last decade.

Now ABC oil drills its first well. The drilling costs in our typical well will total about $10 million from start to finish and will take about a year to complete before it gives us a drop of oil—assuming it WILL give us a drop of oil. We'll have to burn some cash during that year, while rig operators and crews are hired, but no problem, we expected this. At 8 or 9 months, we're getting close to completion, and the results of our drilling are becoming clear. And let's say that we have a winner project, a well that will deliver at least an average amount of oil for a well in a productive U.S. shale play.

So far, so good. We're able to book an excellent return of $80 a barrel in 2011. In the first three months at this price, we'll book more than $2 million (300b/d x 90 days x $80/barrel). Now we're cooking. We're able to pay our debt for the previous year from the bonds we've sold ($10m x 7% = $700,000), and still have plenty of cash to pay all of our other obligations for the next year coming.

The next three months are even better, even if the production numbers start to slip a little towards month six. We'll book perhaps another $1.5 million, enough to either pay down some of our initial debt, or sink some cash into the next well we're planning on developing, or give back some profits to early investors or officers of our fledgling company. Early success with our first well has made financing for the next one even easier, and we'll likely not bother to retire debt that's not due for a decade or more.

We're ready to start on the next well, developing it really close to the first and hoping for similar results. As we continue to drill wells very near the spot where we put our first well, we'll likely see very similar results and very similar economics. Excellent money will flow initially from these wells, which will deliver money for the next project. To our investors, we're going to be a big winner in the shale game.

But the truth is somewhat different: Our first well is going to take a long time to pay off the costs for itself, while it will *look* like it will do it in a matter of months. Its initial returns mask the fact that the well will be nearly powerless by year three. Instead, it will be the initial returns of the 2nd well, and the 3rd and 4th, that will continue to drive the cash flow of the company and retire the initial start-up debt we took on for well #1. On the books, it'll look like the company is making immense returns on their production efforts, when in fact the profits on each individual well are very modest indeed, even at near $100 oil. This is not because the wells aren't exciting and profitable—it's because they are *almost immediately* exciting and profitable.

And what were the final results of our fledgling well? As time moved along, the production numbers continued to disintegrate, and by year three, the well is hardly delivering much cash flow at all. The overall results for our first well are still very worthwhile, but they're no longer as impressive as they might have looked at the start. In three years, averaging, let's say, a very generous 150 barrels a day, our well has made us almost $13 million, a 30% investment rate of return (IRR) in three years—which is nice, but not the 50-70% return that seemed to be promised by the early flow rate.

But if we're running ABC Oil, we're not going to concentrate on making clear the returns on any one well through its lifetime to investors and Wall Street analysts; instead, we're going to emphasize the profits we're amassing from the entire portfolio of wells, or even more impressively the profit stream from next year's portfolio of wells—a return that is only achievable by continuing to increase drilling and production numbers.

In essence, this is the pattern of almost every shale

operator in existence: an endless chase of production increases and greater cash flow to help pay for financing costs and keep the analysts and investors on Wall Street happy. Of course, the mountain of debt you must accumulate to do this is tomorrow's headache. It's a treadmill that's difficult for shale producers to get off of, once it's started. And during the 'easy money' days of 2009-2014, the temptation was overwhelmingly to get on the ride and start running.

SHALE PLAYERS FALTER FAST WHEN THE PRICE OF OIL DROPS

Using this example and now knowing how the shale industry has been constructed, we can see that the biggest problem that any shale player could have would be a sudden drop in the price of oil. The built-in need for constantly increasing drilling activity makes them far more vulnerable than other traditional oil producers to a downward price cycle. A drop in oil prices will equally drop returns and push further forward our projected payoff times and reduce our cash flow, which drives everything else, including our crucial exploration budget. This pattern is true for all oil companies in general, but it's far more critical for shale players because of the front-loaded production we demonstrated earlier in the chapter and their need to continually drill anew.

And perhaps even more important, a drop in oil prices does not incentivize a shale producer to cut back on his drilling and production, as any drop in profitability in any other business would do. It would be a natural business instinct to cut back on production of anything if the profitability falls, wouldn't it? You'd think so. But even besides the 'Ponzi scheme' nature of shale, there are three other roadblocks to shale producers just turning off oil wells when times get tough.

First, most leases in oil and gas are written with a commitment to the lessee of constantly drilling and producing oil and gas from that land. That clause in most drill leases correctly protects lessors by preventing oil companies from merely snapping up acreage to keep it away from competitors and hold it indefinitely without working it. With those clauses in place, oil companies have an immediate responsibility to deliver to lessees a return on their contracts. This does keep oil E+P's honest in their negotiations for leases. However, the downside for the oil producer, the lessee, and even the market in general is that oil producers contractually have a tough time halting their pumping when market conditions become unprofitable, or if they simply run out of capital.

Secondly, even when a well has been correctly planned and drilled and then temporarily abandoned because of a cratering market or a lack of capital, it does not just sit there waiting to be revived. Shale wells typically cannot be 'brought back to life' whenever the markets and the driller can justify it. Most technologies for fracking require an expense almost equivalent to the original investment to renew a previously abandoned well. Those renewal costs make shutting down a project in midstream economically impractical, no matter where oil prices are.

A third roadblock to cutting back production is with Wall Street, which typically rates oil companies based on increasing production over everything else. Capital support, credit ratings, investor interest, and stock prices for an oil company all rely on a driller continuing to show a solid increase in production numbers, year after year.

But even besides all of these disincentives to stop drilling, the financial need to keep the lights on with cash flow at all costs is the most overwhelming. It's clear that the lower oil prices go, instead of cutting back production, a driller needs to produce ever more and not less. He is constantly hounded by trying to always generate at least an equivalent cash flow, no matter the prices of oil and gas in the market, as his accumulated credit and bond debt doesn't take a holiday, just because the markets are down.

It's an insane Catch-22 that strangely incentivizes shale producers to pump more and more oil precisely when the profits on that oil are marginal at best, or even negative. We can see this clearly in the charts for U.S. production we displayed previously (Figures 3.1 and 3.3), which show a steady increase in the amount of oil being pumped by U.S. shale players no matter where the price of oil is. Up market or down market, it doesn't matter: shale players are constantly hounded to keep their spigots at full open and be constantly working to get the next well to start flowing, and the next and the next. Just to continue to survive, they have their amplifiers, in the immortal words of *Spinal Tap,* always turned up to eleven.

Figure 6.5.
U.S. Shale Oil Company Bankruptcies (2015-2020)

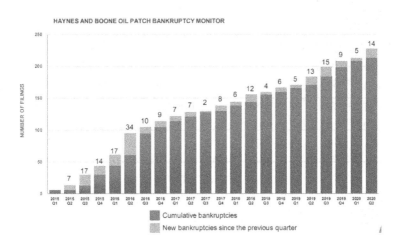

This is a crazy economic drumbeat for a whole industry to march to. It doesn't make much sense. You'd think that with this treadmill of production, and with the bust in oil prices that began in 2014 and have continued to this day, and with the natural laws of economics we all know so well, we'd have seen a complete decimation of the shale oil industry by now. And indeed, there have been many, many bankruptcies and restructurings during that time. More than 200 companies in oil and gas have declared Chapter 11 since 2015. But there have been few large companies that have gone away in that time. Why is that?

The answer lies both in the ready mountain of cash that has been willing to pour into shale, which we've already examined, but also in the immense improvements in well geology, spacing, fracking cocktails, cementing, and other well services advances that we've seen since 2010. The first place that immense improvement is evident is in Figure 6.5 above, where the initial volumes of fracked wells has increased exponentially. While some of this improvement is attributable to the erosion of lesser-quality shale plays from practical oil production, the advances in fracking technologies to production enhancement cannot be underestimated.

These improvements were an obvious and tremendous boon for all shale oil E&Ps and their long-term viability. For our imaginary oil company, ABC might see 300 barrels a day in the first 3 months of typical well production in 2011, while initial volumes would have increased 20% or more every year since.

With increasing initial results from better technology and concurrent increases in projected reserves by official agencies like the Energy Information Agency (EIA), how can I possibly be calling the shale oil revolution a Ponzi scheme?

Not only does the EIA believe in the continued ramping up of tight oil production well into the next decade, it is even convinced of the potential of increasing efficiencies on conventional supplies here in the U.S., which have done nothing but *decrease* since the 1970s. This is a fantasy swallowed whole by Wall Street and U.S. investors. No, despite all the good news, shale is still inevitably headed for a production cliff. It's just well shrouded and tougher to see as the boom times are going on.

But let's look a bit further into the future and try to remove some of the shrouds. First, we have seen that there are only a few core areas of shale worth working here in the U.S., and they're all being relentlessly tapped right now. It's also inevitable that efficiency and technological advances in drilling for shale oil won't forever make up for the quantifiable limits of prime shale acreage. And when the final potential of technology improvements is reached, which would seem to be soon, the truth of just how much good shale acreage there is out there will be far more obvious than it is now. In fact, what has lately begun to take hold is an idea that I wrote about in my last book in 2015: That this kind of really rich, profitable acreage is far from endless and actually very limited indeed. In fact, I believe we have already reached the peak of U.S. production potential, or are very, very near to it. Even our old friend Harold Hamm of Continental Resources warned correctly about this in 2017 when he predicted that many shale producers were likely to "drill themselves into oblivion." It seems that's precisely what they've done—and despite his own warning, we can't exempt Hamm and Continental Resources itself, either.

Front-loading of shale production is one reason I think shale oil has some of the attributes of a Ponzi scheme—inspiring increased capital injections based on very exciting initial results that cannot be maintained. Interpolating the progress of U.S. oil production based on recent improvements in fracking technology and believing the fantasy that those improvements will always continue, ad infinitum, is another.

But we're pretty clearly already reaching a tipping point. U.S. shale production is seen to be emptying most of the really productive acreage in the U.S. The peak of production is already long past in the Bakken, and it's just beginning to drop from its apex in the Eagle Ford. That's two of the three of the 'hottest' U.S. shale plays, and the third, the Permian, is showing all the same first symptoms of its coming decline as the other two. As we move farther along, shale production will inevitably consist of ever-less-productive wells that cost more to drill, take longer to pay themselves off, and generate less oil.

The differences in shale production compared to all other types of oil production cannot be overemphasized if we are to understand the current oil markets and how to fix them, to allow for a more rapid entry of natural gas and renewables. Yes, it is true that every well, whether fracked or not, ultimately decays to zero. But shale is different. Shale wells get used up at a rate almost 10 times faster than other oil projects and therefore force shale oil producers into constantly chasing more activity in successively less and less promising acreage, just to stay even. That is entirely unique, and ultimately unsustainable.

In order to actually grow, shale oil companies need an absolutely furious pace of investment and drilling, paying off early investors and bondholders, attracting new investors, and spending ever more capital. That outline for continued success sounds familiar in many ways to me. It sounds much like a typical Ponzi scheme.

It has become finally clear to investors (and bond holders) that this kind of open tap to capital that many U.S. shale producers have been able to continually access has not been particularly successful for anyone. Sure, oil company officers and CEOs have been able to give themselves tremendous salaries and increasing bonuses for increasing production year after year—which is the only metric they've been held to for success by Wall Street in the past. But the two years of 2018 and 2019 have proven to investors how ultimately pointless continued capital investment has turned out with most over-leveraged shale oil companies. We've seen much of this credit and appetite of both private funds and individual investors disappearing, as they begin to demand returns as opposed to mere production increases.

But much of the problem is hard to fix, at least by merely cutting off many oil companies from their capital lifelines. There is an old saying that if you owe the bank $10,000, they own you, but if you owe them $10 million, you own the bank. For years, bond holders have continued to dribble capital into even the worst of these producers, keeping their oil production businesses alive—that cash flow being the only way to recoup any of their investments. There have been countless cases of oil companies going bankrupt, only to have bankruptcy courts demand that they continue to keep the lights on and the oil flowing, again to satisfy somewhat the bondholders demanding some few pennies of return on their dollar investments. Now, that's the worst kind of Ponzi Scheme: one where even the victims are forced to continue playing, even after they know they've been duped.

Two conflicting but consistent themes continue to haunt shale oil drilling. One, seen by the Haynes and Boone chart in Figure 6.5, makes clear that shale oil companies continue to be under stress and go bankrupt despite where oil prices are trading—unless those prices are very, very high indeed. In fact, the rate of bankruptcies has been steady since the bust of 2014, when oil prices sank below $100 a barrel.

The second is even more telling. Oil production here in the United States, despite depressed prices for the past 5 years, and the clearly uneconomic profit margins of new production, still continues to rise, inexorably.

No matter how you characterize the nature of the shale oil (and gas) industry in the United States, the most important thing to realize is how all aspects of the development of that business—when it rose, how it gained steam, what its general financial form is, and how it is organized to make profits—impact the way that the entirety of the global oil market is currently structured and operates. It is critical to note that shale oil operators have all (to one degree or another) fallen into a trap of cheap credit, driving an ever-expanding business model of ever-growing production to pay for production already completed and early investors expecting a return.

It's not that the production of shale oil might not be profitable; in many areas of the United States, using a model of more traditional financing and far more dependable expectations of returns, fracking for oil can be another production path that can be at least as profitable as more conventional oil production both onshore and off, if not more so. It seems that the consolidation of much of the best acreage in the United States over the years following the latest price bust of 2014—into the hands of the larger independents and especially multi-national mega-cap majors—will portend a future where shale oil is produced using far more discipline, far less leveraged debt, and far more reasonable expectations for profits.

But that is not the current state of a large percentage of shale production now, nor was it the state of the vast majority of shale production in the 'glory days' from 2009-2014, when the tidal wave of new supply from shale disrupted the global supply marketplace from its 'natural' course of ever-higher prices.

That glut in the marketplace, caused by shale players who must continually pump more and more oil in order to stay afloat, has also been exceedingly slow to clear. Even as I write these words in 2020, the EIA is predicting over a million barrels a day of more oil to appear from shale this year alone, and at least another 300,000 barrels a day in 2021. (Update: Before coronavirus).

Now, I may think that the EIA is wrong in its predictions, but that doesn't matter much; it is the nature of the way that shale oil production has been structured here in the U.S. to expect such an increase to consistently occur, whether or not the marketplace—and its prices particularly—justify it. The only thing that might stop it is a vast increase in bankruptcies, at an even greater rate than has been seen since 2015.

But this model of ever-increasing barrels from U.S. shale, only slowed, momentarily, by the sharp blade of a bankruptcy court is simply an inefficient and stupid way of allocating our precious domestic resources, as well as being an equally ridiculous model of running a business, for the supposed benefit of markets and shareholders alike. Something has to change, if we are to get to grips with this wholly disruptive oil-producing sub-sector on global markets. If we're ever to turn around the ever-growing demand for fossil fuels worldwide towards more carbon neutral sources, we're going to have to find a way to get oil prices up, which U.S. shale producers have made impossible since they arrived after the financial crisis, and will continue to make impossible if we allow it.

CHAPTER 7:

CORONAVIRUS: THE UNEXPECTED OIL DISASTER

As I spent the better part of a year writing this book, I thought that most of the controversy it was likely to cause was my fierce disgust of the U.S. oil industry and specifically its approach to oil fracking over the last 10 years. I have posited that the oil industry's behavior has been the single most influential roadblock—worldwide—to more environmentally friendly energy. Economically speaking, I haven't been shy throughout this book to say that the fracking of oil in the United States stands (to me) as the most craven, self-indulgent, undisciplined, and truly criminal waste of both a limited sovereign natural resource and investor money as any capitalist endeavor perhaps in the history of the world.

I've also said previously that the independent oil companies here in the United States did not perpetrate this crime against our environment and their investors without help: no one could manage such a disastrous feat all on their own. No, they had a ton of help from both the Federal and State governments and their mostly laissez-faire regulatory stance toward frackers that encouraged unrestricted expansion and the waste that came with it, hypercharged after 2017 by the Trump administration's rollbacks on regulation.

Even more, they found that they had access to a nearly unlimited flow of cheap capital, courtesy of the very low interest rates that the Federal Reserve never had the courage and good sense to raise, despite the fact that the economic crisis that had spurred that once-critical and unprecedented policy was nearly 10 years past. Especially with Wall Street banks as well as private and individual investors, those low interest rates generated an equally undisciplined search for returns outside of low-paying bonds, and they randomly flung money at just about any marginally reasonable business plan they could find in the oil patch, whether from established firms or fly-by-night fracking start-ups.

Oil companies greedily sucked up all of this money, delivering nothing more than ever-increasing volumes of crude oil for it, while spiraling ever more into debt. That's the simple, one-sentence explanation of what has happened in the oil patch with shale over the last 10 years. Oil companies gave investors "growth" (or at least the look of it) instead of a return on invested capital, and the Wall Street analysts—instead of recognizing the Ponzi-scheme spiral this behavior was perpetuating, asking hard questions, demanding better planning, and then downgrading the companies who were abusing this trust the most—instead patted the oil companies' executives on the back and gave them high marks for their investor clients to read (at least until late in 2019).

Meanwhile, the oil executives didn't mind at all using this singular metric of growth to pay themselves ever more, based solely on the increases in oil production that all their borrowed money had inspired and not on the balance sheets they oversaw—balance sheets that consistently, for nearly a decade, got ever worse. As companies went ever more into debt, management teams, instead of seeing this downward spiral of financing as a warning sign that needed repair, instead counted the increasing numbers of barrels they were adding to the global marketplace as the lone success to be rewarded for.

Throughout all of this, their pipe-dream escape plan remained universally the same: a gospel to keep faith in throughout all of this stupidity: All you ever needed to right the ship, no matter how deeply in debt you got, was an oil price that went and stayed above $80 a barrel. Even I will admit that through the first few years of the oil price collapse, this didn't seem like much to ask for; we'd seen triple-digit, or near-triple-digit, oil prices through most of the 2000s as well as the first four years of the 2010s, until 2014. With demand numbers for oil continuing to increase worldwide, it all seemed to every expert in the oil patch like nothing more than a matter of time before the markets bailed everyone out, as it had time and time again before. All you really needed to see it through was a way to stay alive, keep pumping and survive.

And how do you do that? Well, it wouldn't take much, considering the economic landscape of the times: just a steady flow of fresh capital or a respectable cash flow to keep all the juggling pins of bonds, leases, and loans in the air. Just make it to the next boom, they said, the next inevitable boom in a long history of recurring oil booms: get there before all those pins came crashing to the floor at once. At least, that is what most in the oil patch told themselves.

And then the coronavirus hit.

THE CORONAVIRUS CHANGES EVERYTHING IN THE OIL PATCH

There aren't many silver linings to be gleaned from this global pandemic. But one of the few was the stark relief under which the U.S. oil and gas industry was subjected to because of it. All veils, rationalizations, and hopeful thoughts were wiped away in an instant, leaving U.S. frackers en masse like the emperor without clothes: naked, vulnerable, and embarrassed.

When the first reports of a new respiratory virus emerged from the industrial province of Wuhan in China, very few could possibly grasp just how massive a global impact it was about to have. Even as I update this section in late 2020, it seems that the most difficult economic trials of this pandemic are still months away from being felt. But the quick expansion of the outbreak and the accompanying number of hospitalizations and deaths, once the virus was discovered on every continent on the globe, delivered some unprecedented economic hardships unlike any other downturn ever seen before.

The lock-down that was executed in China helped to quickly control the numbers of cases (within 4 months) and deaths there, but it was clear that the tools that were available to the Chinese were not as readily available to other Western, democratic nations. Whereas the Chinese were able to place a 'cordon sanitaire' around an entire city where the outbreaks were most rapid, in other Western nations, where free movement and free assembly are considered inalienable rights, the governments' reaction was far slower and less responsive to the outbreak. This then allowed the spread of the virus to move unchecked for several weeks, perhaps months, until slowly but surely the entire rest of the free world, first in Italy and then in the UK and U.S., was forced to stop all human interactions of more than a few people. Commerce of all kinds came to a screaming halt, the kind of decline in economic activity that even the Great Depression or the financial crisis of 2008 hadn't seen.

OPEC AND RUSSIA REACT

In late February 2020, initial expectations for global oil demand were calculated for a drop of perhaps 1.5-2 million barrels a day for the remaining 2nd quarter and 3rd quarter of 2020, although we now know that to have been wildly optimistic. In any case, under these expectations, the Saudis scheduled an emergency meeting of the OPEC cartel, including Russia (the plus sign of the new OPEC+ collective) on March 8th, seeking a 1m -1.5m production cut, designed again to bring the oil markets into relative balance. They had done this before several times in the previous two years, and everyone expected them to do it again. Instead, the Russians balked.

This perhaps shouldn't have come of as much of a surprise, but in fact, it stunned virtually everyone, including me. From 2017 on, OPEC+ had been characterized by a tenuous but mutually useful partnership between the Saudis and the Russians, to take up the slack of excess supply (coming almost entirely from U.S. frackers) in order to keep the oil markets relatively stable. Russia's economic health is tied sharply to oil prices, and in the face of dropping demand from the coronavirus outbreak, most analysts fully expected the Russians would be forced to do pretty much anything the Saudis directed in order to protect prices.

A similarly high oil price is even more important for Saudi Arabia, and not only because its economy relied even more on oil revenues than Russia. The recent Saudi Aramco IPO and continuing hopes to further monetize Saudi oil assets added to Saudi Arabia's desperate need to keep oil prices stabilized.

Previous agreements to adjust production downwards in the prior two years had gone relatively smoothly between the Russians and the Saudis, and few thought that either had much of a choice this time around either but to again bite the bullet and take up the excess supply that U.S. producers had so irresponsibly thrown, once more, onto the global market.

But not this time. What went through the minds of Putin and the Russians was easy to figure out after the moment passed, even though no one managed to predict that it was coming at the time. Russia recognized a real and new vulnerability of U.S. oil producers in the pandemic, who had been—finally—financially crippled in the last year by the capital markets. Beginning in late 2019, private and public investment had dried up, with investors unwilling to continue to lend endless amounts of fresh money for U.S. oil E&Ps to flush down the next fracked well. Indeed, the recent relative restraint of investors in fracking companies had already trimmed stock prices significantly during the late fall of 2018 and into 2019, despite stock indexes that had continue to soar.

In response, oil companies had been forced to begin to show signs of some discipline in restricting capital expense budgets and turning off (or holding in reserve) already fracked wells that weren't profitable at under $50 a barrel. Analysts also began—again, finally—to question the lone benchmark of higher production as success, as opposed to real returns on investor capital. This late-stage discipline from U.S. oil companies turned out to be far too little, too late. Six months of small attempts to trim budgets and throttle back on growth (while not committing to decreasing production at all) couldn't make a significant dent in the vast amounts of debt many of them had accumulated over the previous decade. Only a price of oil floating in the $50s and $60s, along with the cash flow that it brought, had saved many of these firms from bankruptcy already—a vast army of "walking dead" zombie frackers.

None of this went unobserved by the Russians, who recognized in the coronavirus outbreak a unique opportunity to break many of these producers once and for all, and truly put the U.S. "zombies" into their graves. With this long-term determination in mind to eliminate American fracking competition, the Russians refused to budge on further production cuts of their own. Even more simply, the Russians had grown sick and tired of deferring their own oil profits for the benefit of rival U.S. oil companies. In this, it was hard for anyone to argue their point. The Russians had, in fact, put off many new oil development projects and deferred their own growth in production during 2017-2018, only to see U.S. oil production from fracking continue to massively increase instead, from 8 to 9, 10, 11 million barrels a day, and now touching roughly 11.3 million barrels a day in March 2020. The Russians had had enough, and they told the Saudis they wouldn't be part of another cut.

THE SAUDIS DECLARE A PRICE WAR

At first, and perhaps in a real show of anger, the Saudis and MbS didn't hesitate with their reaction.

They saw Russian intransigence as an economic declaration of war.

As if daring the Russians to follow through on their threat, the Saudis announced that they would not unilaterally decrease production by the proposed 1.5m barrels a day. Instead, they announced that they would INCREASE production by at least 2 million barrels a day, and drop their benchmark price—which at the time was trading near $45 a barrel—nearly 50%, to $25 a barrel.

MbS had openly dared the Russians: *"You really want a war for market share? OK then, we'll show you how it's done."*

The response from Russia to this threat of price war was to be expected: they didn't even bother responding. One thing that has been consistent about Vladimir Putin throughout his history is that he responds poorly to threats and ultimatums. Once the policy from Putin had been set, there was little chance that the Saudi prince could make any counter-threat that would have an impact. No matter what economic hardships that months of very low oil prices might inflict on the Russian economy and Russian people, in Russia, it is Putin alone who needs to be satisfied. No public outcry or public display of protest was likely to arise, certainly no Putin-sponsored oligarch was likely to speak up against him, nor any political opponent of any strength likely to emerge. No matter where the ruble might trade for the next several months, or even years, or what levels of unemployment and poverty might emerge in Russia among the Russian people, Putin's voice was, and is, the only one that matters in determining oil policy. Others might suffer, but Putin himself wasn't going to go hungry in the meantime. And in Russia, that's all that matters.

In the futures markets, the prospect of a price war between two of the three largest global suppliers of oil was immediate and brutal: oil got crushed. WTI, already under pressure for most of 2020, having already traded down below $50 from near $64 a barrel, was sent reeling down more than $11, from $46 to $35, a drop of nearly 24%. Coronavirus took care of the rest. The global pandemic forced complete shutdowns in most countries, first in South Korea and Singapore, then in Europe and finally in the United States. This had the global economic effect of an equally huge drop in economic activity, save for food and medical services. All else pretty much stopped. Planes didn't fly, buses and trains had no passengers, movie theaters and auditoriums no patrons, restaurants no diners. The effects were far faster and more devastating than even the collapse in 1929 or 2008 had been, and oil demand was only one casualty of the economic halt.

It's hard to know exactly how much oil demand was removed from the global economy during the first few months of the global pandemic. Oil analysts' estimates ranged as widely as 5 million barrels a day to as much as 30 million barrels a day. The stripping of demand now made whatever additional supply the Saudis or the Russians could possibly put on the market from any kind of price war completely moot.

CORONAVIRUS FINISHES THE 2014 OIL BUST'S JOB

In retrospect, there was no cut at an OPEC March meeting that could have stopped the decimation of oil prices that followed anyway. Demand destruction became the next, even more devastating, 40-ton pressure on oil prices and oil swooned even further, breaking the $20 a barrel threshold briefly in late March, even outstripping the fire-sale $25 a barrel price that the Saudis had set.

In early April 2020, storage for the massive 8 to 25 (or more) barrel-a-day surplus quickly ran out, despite the full use of the U.S. Strategic Petroleum Reserve, other nations' reserve tanks, every ultra large (ULCC) tanker roaming the seas, and perhaps every Saudi and Iranian unfilled bathtub. This made for a unique moment in the history of the oil markets (or at least, any I've ever seen before) when the world was possibly going to run out of places to put added supplies.

And then what would happen? Everyone in the oil world was trying to figure that out. But, if natural gas in the Permian basin of Texas during 2019 was any indication, the market could even price oil below zero. (UPDATE: indeed, oil briefly went negative later that month.) A similar event happened in the bond markets in Japan when its central bank went to negative interest rates: buyers of Japanese bonds had to pay for the government to hold their money.

How can this ever happen? How is it possible for any commodity to have less than no value? Well, when there's more supply than demand, prices go down: we know that. We also know that when prices go down, supply should naturally decrease too. That's another of the basic economic laws and makes intuitive sense: there is a price so cheap that it's not worth it for people to make a product anymore.

But what happens if supply doesn't, or even can't, decrease? That is precisely the case for many oil producers, not only in the United States, but globally. They have to have cash flow today, even if they are constantly losing money on every sale they make. I am curiously watching oil markets in April 2020 in a way I haven't ever before in my 35-year career, expecting a day, perhaps soon, when oil producers will not only get nothing for the oil they produce, but will literally have to pay somebody to have their oil carted away. (UPDATE: I considered rewriting this section after oil futures traded in negative prices later in April 2020, because it frankly sounds far too Svengali-like and self-serving to offer up this possibility after the fact. All it intended to prove at the time was the endemic problem that oil markets have with local storage – and how local pricing dependent on local storage can upset global prices in a very negative (and ridiculous) way.)

Nobody is confidently predicting this; everyone thinks that production will have to stop if oil prices really approach zero. They're probably right: negative oil prices will make for a fast change of behavior from producers. But the unique environment of oil markets, created over the last 10 years and put into overdrive because of the coronavirus pandemic, makes it possible that negative prices could happen.

And that's precisely the point. We know (without any degree in finance) that nobody can sell you something for free—not and survive for long. But the model of many shale producers has been doing EXACTLY THIS for years already: using various forms of credit, as well as public and private investment, to keep their businesses going despite being consistently on the losing side of the profit ledger.

The truth is that they were already going broke; they were just doing it more slowly.

The only difference I am looking at today (in early April 2020) is that this process is about to get a whole lot faster than it has in the past. A whole lot faster. And that means that this moment in history, as devastating as it will be for the oil industry, will also likely be a definitive economic example of what economists call 'creative destruction.'

Creative destruction is fundamental to the theory of free markets and market efficiency. Unfettered capitalism says that markets alone are capable of deciding the 'good' companies from the bad ones and should bear the burden of rewarding profitable businesses, while punishing those that aren't.

In oil, producers should enter a marketplace as long as they can make a profit after buying the equipment and manpower they need, paying to lease acreage, drilling, and transporting their product to market. Fundamental economics say that if too many players enter this market, prices will decrease from competition. And if the prices decrease enough, it will naturally force out the least-efficient or the less-well-capitalized players. This is the 'creative' part of the destruction: creative in that the marketplace naturally chooses the 'best' producers of any product.

Now, let's add some fundamental economic supply-and-demand laws to our markets and see how creative destruction should work in practice. Anything that adds supply to the markets more quickly should accelerate destruction by driving prices lower more quickly. In shale, we've noted the unprecedented access to capital, an endless supply of investor 'lifelines' for even bad shale players. However, for those investors, no matter whether they have partnered with these 'losers' or merely own their stocks and bonds, they are punished with a less-than-adequate or even a negative return on their investments. As they learn their lessons over time, investors naturally withdraw from these 'less-than-best' companies. Withholding of investment chokes these less capable oil companies of the money they need to operate and expand, accelerating their demise even further. As these less-profitable companies disappear, the better-run, better-capitalized players remaining will be left to take advantage of the better prices that this weeding out of competition will bring.

In this example, the market incentives of investment and free price discovery were the only inputs into this process. Conservative economists will rejoice at this example: Capitalism has been proven to be the 'best' system of allocating resources. We've seen this happen once already in the shale patch, in 2015-2017, where several hundred small shale players fell victim to the price bust.

But the most important point to be drawn here is that this creative destruction process for shale oil has been painstakingly slow, inadequate, and incomplete. Despite the number of bankruptcies we've seen in the oil patch, the 'destruction' that was needed to truly rebalance markets and reward the disciplined producers while removing the 'losers' as we moved past 2016 never fully happened. And as we entered 2020, we were set with much of the same environment of overproducing, undisciplined shale players as we had entering 2014.

But with the coronavirus outbreak, we had an unprecedented global decrease in demand, to levels not seen since the 1990s, supercharging creative destruction like never before.

Figure 7.1.
Coronavirus Causes Oil Demand to Hit the Skids

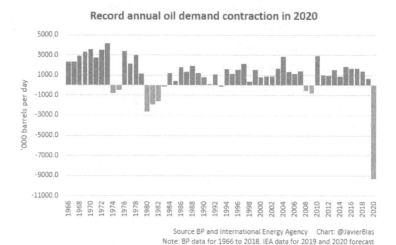

Record annual oil demand contraction in 2020

Source BP and International Energy Agency   Chart: @JavierBlas
Note: BP data for 1966 to 2018. IEA data for 2019 and 2020 forecast

Remember, both increasing supply and decreasing demand are really two sides of the same coin. But, decreasing demand is usually even more powerful than increasing supply, because it can be so rapid and massive, as we've seen during recessions, financial crises, and now a new force, global pandemics, as seen in Figure 7.1. Decreasing demand shrinks the market and the number of folks willing to buy your product, in essence doing the same thing as increasing available supply.

In this case, the drop in global demand was estimated at nearly 30 million barrels a day during the height of the COVID-19 crisis, and predicted to be more than 9 million barrels a day on average for 2020—and the crisis didn't even take hold until March. Contrast this to the 2 million barrels a day that the Russians and Saudis were pushing forward in their short-lived price war to crater prices. This kind of instantaneous decrease in demand is something that the energy markets have never seen before, not even during the financial crisis of 2008. Add that to an ongoing price war and added supply surplus, and you're going to have an example of 'creative destruction' run amok.

Keep this idea of creative destruction, Capitalist theory, and 'winners' and 'losers' in mind as we proceed through the rest of this chapter. We'll need it, and we'll return to it soon.

HOW THE CORONAVIRUS IS DESTROYING OIL COMPANIES

Meanwhile as I write this, I'm beginning to see some of this ac-celerated 'creative destruction' from the coronavirus crisis be-ginning. In late March 2020, Whiting Resources, one of the largest producers of shale oil in the once preeminent Bakken oil fields of South Dakota, filed for Chapter 11. The massive stock market decline of oil stocks' value in March 2020 pointed to many once well-capitalized oil companies—now trading in sin-gle digits or even pennies—that were now likely to follow Whit-ing out the door. But here's where 'free-market' capitalism and its neat theories came off the rails during the pandemic. Shale executives, facing bankruptcy, began to beg Washington to do something to help them—and add them to the list of 'essential' U.S. businesses needing support during the outbreak.

Key among the corporate supplicants was Harold Hamm, whose company, Continental Resources, is the largest shale oil pro-ducer in the Bakken. Hamm is a trusted Trump friend once thought to be the most likely Energy Department chief (before Rick Perry was named). In an appearance on Bloomberg on March 11th, Hamm asked the Commerce department to investi-gate the Saudis about 'illegal' dumping of oil and tanking of prices calculated to put him and other shale companies out of business. And although he claimed that Continental was well capitalized and "not looking for a bailout," he did say that a

Federal loan program for "some companies in the sector could be helpful." According to Reuters reporting, Hamm was hardly alone in reaching out to the White House for the help they desperately needed to survive.

Trump has had an obsession throughout his political life with low oil prices, equating them with political success (as I have mentioned previously). In the midst of a reelection season, the fast bankrupting of U.S. independent energy sector, with its many dependent multi-billion-dollar sub-sectors also in danger, was impossible for Trump to leave to its own fate. Besides having many of his friends committed to oil, hundreds of thousands of jobs in Pennsylvania, Texas, and Oklahoma remained at stake. But Trump was facing a difficult choice as so many U.S. companies were in equal, if not greater, distress. Airlines, hotels, and other recreational businesses faced disaster as well, and did not have nearly the 'baggage' of poor public support nor shared as much blame for causing their own problems as U.S. oil. Further, an outright bailout to big oil companies couldn't merit their desperate need while hundreds of thousands of small businesses were imploding and individuals were filing for unemployment in record numbers. In April 2020 alone, U.S. unemployment spiked from 3.5% to 16%.

Instead of offering subsidized loans or an outright bailout, Trump called on the Saudi prince to make a deal with the Russians and put the price war to an end. And while both the Saudis and the Russians liked what basement oil prices were doing to their U.S. counterparts, MbS and the Saudis simply couldn't afford to ignore the request of any U.S. President. On Easter Sunday, April 12th, ministers from all the OPEC countries, Russia, and the United States met remotely to hammer out an amazing collective effort: a production cut of 10 million barrels a day, extended with some limitations, through 2021. As stunning as this agreement was, it brought up a nest of very thorny questions for the United States, as well as the rest of the OPEC+ cartel.

First was the math of the cut itself. With a surplus of nearly 30 million barrels in April filling global storage rapidly, the timeline for the 100% utilization of every tank and reserve supply was estimated to be as early as June. With that information known, it seemed hardly much of a concession for both the Saudis and the Russians to agree to even this desperate a cut, as there was soon to be literally no place left to put the stuff.

Second was the new U.S. engagement with the OPEC cartel. While acting as a mediator, Trump had offered the natural drop in U.S. production that was estimated by the EIA of 2m barrels a day as the U.S. 'contribution' towards the 10-million-barrel cut. But at the last minute of negotiations, Trump offered to withhold an additional 300,000 barrels a day from U.S. production, after the Mexican oil minister refused to commit to his requested quota. With that commitment, the United States became, for the first time, an active participant in the OPEC cartel, in essence joining with a global manipulator of oil prices. Conservative economists were going to have a hard time squaring this new policy with their American capitalist doctrine—as well as raising a myriad of questions as to how deeply the U.S. government could exert its influence going forwards on oil production in the United States.

Finally, and for our purposes, this 'deal' involving the U.S. brought all sorts of risks of moral hazard for oil companies into greater focus. Remember the idea of creative destruction and allowing the markets alone to pick winners and losers? With Trump's purposeful thumb pushing on the pricing scale, the United States threw U.S. producers a stronger lifeline than any other straightforward bailout: it had actively engaged in pushing oil prices higher for the benefit of oil company profits and the detriment of U.S. consumers. Trump had given shale 'losers' another chance to be winners.

And it is unclear whether this will be the only relief that the Federal government will hand to oil companies. In response to the pandemic, the U.S. government embarked on the largest dollar programs for propping up the U.S. economy ever seen. The first stimulus program approved by Congress amounted to more than $2 trillion. In comparison, the 2009 American Recovery and Reinvestment Act was a 'measly' $787 billion. Further, The Federal Reserve, virtually unlimited in its ability to buy debt, indicated it would buy assets of all kinds— as it did in 2008, and has expanded its balance sheet in assets far more than in 2009—to a gargantuan $16 trillion (update: Treasury debt exceeded $20.5 trillion as of August 2020, exceeding the current Gross National Product). This commitment dwarfs the purchase of failed mortgages the Federal Reserve made during the credit crisis. It seems highly likely that a good portion of those assets that will be bought will be precisely the high-yield, high-risk bonds of many of the most leveraged shale oil companies of Texas, Oklahoma, Arkansas, and the Dakotas.

What all this means for oil in the short term is difficult to know. While even a 10m-barrel-a-day cut would seem to remove some of the worst predictions for oil prices falling into single-digits or even negative territory, the oil markets barely reacted to the deal after it was struck and soon began sinking again towards $20 a barrel. Ten million barrels is an enormous amount, but it still is a long way from the 30m-barrel-a-day surplus that will likely continue through the summer of 2020.

No matter whether this 'deal' can be adhered to or not, and even after the balance of supply and demand is put in relative equality, there will still be an enormous overhang of surplus oil that will surely keep a lid on global prices for at least an extra year, if not two. This almost-certain low oil price that we'll see through 2020, 2021, and perhaps part of 2022 will do a lot of the 'creative destruction' we should be hoping to see, clearing out many of the badly run oil producers here in the United States. But even with this, the two-pronged support of Trump and the Federal government of the oil 'deal' and asset purchases will allow far too many of these 'zombies' to continue to limp on a lot longer than they should otherwise.

So the long-term effect of the coronavirus on the oil markets—and our prospects for a renewable future—is unfortunately far more predictable. Oil will stay cheap longer, a lot longer than it should. The timeline I considered six months ago as reasonable, with national initiatives (of hopefully the next administration) pushing oil prices to move naturally higher, has again, unexpectedly, been delayed. However, this one can't be blamed on the oil companies, for a change.

But the results are unfortunately similar. While the many long-term effects of coronavirus will be felt in our society and economy for many years to come, this effect—of another delay in the natural evolution towards renewables—will be the least appreciated, but likely most dangerous one, for the planet we live on.

CHAPTER 8:

CORONAVIRUS 2: THE DISASTER THAT DOESN'T END

E vents change quickly during the age of coronavirus, that's for sure. No sooner had I finished writing the previous chapter on the impacts of the first few weeks of the outbreak on oil markets and oil producers than another crazy moment required me to write more about it. And I'm sure no matter when I finish, I'll be insufficiently describing the effects of COVID-19 on oil—no less than on the global economy at large.

But you've got to stop somewhere. Also, in the last 48 hours, I've witnessed two significant events: first, the pricing of oil barrels in negative numbers, and second, the promise of President Trump to deliver an industry-wide bailout to oil companies. If those two events don't define everything that's wrong with the oil industry and prove how destructive they've been to our goals of energy evolution and the rise of renewables, I don't know what could.

HOW CAN NEGATIVE PRICING EVEN HAPPEN?

Although I wrote about the possibility of negative pricing of oil in Chapter 7, it's hard to imagine just what it means for a commodity to be priced in negative numbers. It's completely

bizarre, as if you went into a deli to order a roast beef sand-
wich, and the counterman handed you a five-dollar bill with
your order. It sounds utterly ridiculous for anybody to be willing to pay you to take away a thing of value. However, even
though its rarer than hens' teeth, not only is it possible when
you're talking about commodities, it has happened before—
and in energy, no less.

The last time was fairly recently, during the summer of 2019,
when natural gas coming out of West Texas was priced in negative numbers, a gross mismanagement of our national resources to actually have an energy source of any kind be priced
more cheaply than zero. But the circumstances regarding natural gas in Texas in 2019 and oil being delivered in May 2020
at Cushing, Oklahoma, had a lot in common.

It has to do with storage. With natural gas in Texas (as I will
explain in Chapter 10 on natural gas), lack of storage in that
case was a lack of pipelines outfitted to take natural gas to
market. As we will discover in Chapter 10, that was a deliberate construct of the oil and pipeline companies, as they were
maneuvering to get at more profitable oil coming out of their
wells, and treat the associated natural gas in those wells as a
waste product. In that case, with nowhere for the natural gas
to go, prices traded on the physical markets in the red, mean-
ing you really DID have to pay someone to take the natural gas
away, if you wanted it off your hands.

The coronavirus created a less-orchestrated, but more basic
supply/demand case in West Texas Intermediate oil futures
contracts in May. With collapsing demand of 30 million barrels a day and 'only' a 10-million-barrel-a-day commitment of
cut production coming from the combined efforts of OPEC+
and the United States in the month of March 2020, the global
oil markets were subjected to a daily surplus of 20 million barrels a day of oil sloshing around during April. With such a
massive surplus and no buyers for all that oil, the barrels only

had one place to go: into storage (you cannot invisibly 'vent' oil like you can natural gas). That storage took traditional forms first (in terminal tanks of known facilities all over the world), but after much of those traditional outlets were filled, oil needed to seek more 'creative' storage solutions, including transport tankers, rail cars, and trucks.

You might ask a few questions here. First, why would anyone produce oil that has no buyers? I think I've explained why sovereign nations like Saudi Arabia and Russia have to pump oil to float their economies, as well as giving several reasons why U.S. producers can't turn off their taps so easily as well. You might also ask why anyone would buy oil they can't use and pay to store either. That's another question that's worth exploring, but later in the chapter. As with all things in the oil markets, there's money to be made in very wild market conditions—for example, if you can find storage in an environment of temporary surplus, a situation called *a carry trade*. But let's talk about that after we describe the weird situation that coronavirus created in the WTI May 2020 oil contract.

A BRIEF BACKGROUND ON TRADING OIL FUTURES

Oil futures are traded in *contracts*, with each month being a separate instrument. If you want to make or take delivery of real oil barrels at the end of the month of April, you will buy or sell a contract of May futures. On the last day of that contract's expiration, you establish the final price of that contract, called the *settlement*, that says exactly how much you must pay or will get for that oil. Further abiding by the contract specifications, you are also required to exchange those physical barrels of oil at a specified place: with the CME's (NYMEX) West Texas Intermediate (WTI) contract that I traded for 25 years, that place is a small oil terminal in Cushing, Oklahoma.

OK: we've got WTI oil contracts for every month of the year, and on expiration we have to either take or make delivery of that oil in Oklahoma, dependent on whether we bought the contract or sold it. But, of course, we didn't buy that contract or sell it in order to make or take delivery at all; in fact, very few other people did, either. Oil futures are mostly a financial instrument, not a physical one, where for all the time before expiration, people are trading millions of contracts, but the only thing changing hands is money, and the only thing the vast majority of the traders *want* to change hands is money— not a drop of the underlying oil. In fact, more than 98% of oil contracts are traded with no desire to either make or take delivery, but merely to either 'hedge' one's exposure to the price of oil (common if you're an oil producer or user and a small percentage of the volume), or to speculate on where oil prices are going (the vast majority of the volume). The truth is, most of the folks trading oil contracts wouldn't know a barrel of oil from a barrel of monkeys (Full disclosure: neither would I.) I went through the mechanism of all this in far greater detail in my first book, *Oil's Endless Bid*, if you're looking for a more complete explanation.

The important point for us is that when contracts finally get to expiration, the reckoning of a financial instrument about to become a physical one becomes more and more real. When futures contracts are about to 'get real' and turn back into physical obligations, the entire game changes. And if you're one of the 98% of folks trading oil contracts that are about to require actual oil to settle—and not just dollars—you're going to have a greater and greater incentive to get out of those contracts before the clock runs out and those contracts expire— which is precisely when your safe exit will expire with them. So, with all that in mind, fast forward to the end of the May 2020 contract in WTI oil: the last two days, in fact.

A SURPLUS OF OIL POSES INTERESTING PROBLEMS FOR FUTURES MARKETS

As I explained in Chapter 7, up to 30 million barrels a day of excess oil began sloshing around the global marketplace at the start of the coronavirus outbreak, while the OPEC+ and U.S. 'consortium' were only able to come up with a 10-million-barrel-a-day production cut. That makes for 20 million barrels a day of surplus oil with no place to go and no one to burn it. In a marketplace for global oil that can move significantly if oil supply and demand get out of balance for even a million barrels a day, this represented an unheard-of surplus crashing onto the market. What to do with all that extra oil? Well, until producers decide to cut production, which you know is easier said than done, you've got nothing you can do but put it into storage.

Storage is a lousy, low-margin business. But on rare occasions like this, people will pay a hefty premium for it, All of a sudden, everyone needs a place to put excess oil, and every kind of storage that was available began filling up, fast. In Cushing, storage tanks reached a previously unheard-of 85% of capacity in the last two days of the May 2020 contract, making that traditional storage option inaccessible to most of the folks still long (on the buy side of contracts). If you were a fund, an ETF, or even a private speculator who was holding contracts, you had little choice but to try and find another buyer to take these contracts off your hands, and you had precious limited time to do it.

But who was going to buy the contracts from you? If you didn't have access to Cushing storage, or another storage option, you couldn't do anything with them, either. The only folks able to buy contracts in the last two days of April were commercial players who already had established lines of credit and storage, and those people were very few and far between.

Because of this, oil prices for that contract began to collapse rapidly—not only down to zero, but actually below it, actually trading more than a negative $35 dollars a barrel (!). It turned out to be a rightfully bizarre and very short-term fluke occurrence. When the smoke cleared that day, creative oil people found all sorts of storage solutions they could use to take advantage of the disconnect, and oil traded up nearly $50 the next day—to a still dirt-cheap (but positive) $15 a barrel.

Sure, this crazy event was an anomaly of the futures markets' mechanism, only possible when a commodity futures contract is about to expire with desperate 'stuck' owners of contracts searching for buyers and no ready storage available. And much of the blame for the lack of options for storage can be laid on the contract itself, written for a small inland terminal like Cushing, and not for a coastline delivery point on the Gulf, for example. And finally, the CME exchange probably had an obligation to step in and mediate the outcome of the contract once all trading had come off the rails and delivered such unrealistically negative prices. All of that is surely true.

But to dismiss this event as a unique one without deeper repercussions for the oil markets in general is to miss the point. Negative pricing of oil (even for a brief moment in a unique situation) says something more about the bankruptcy of the current oil markets and the system of futures and physical pricing. It also makes a point about the mistaken priorities of energy policy and the unrealistic and unnecessary goals of U.S. energy independence that makes it even possible for physical gluts and storage issues so deep like this to happen in the first place.

Throughout this book, I have been trying to show that, before the onset of the effects of the coronavirus pandemic, the global oil marketplace, and particularly the players, incentives, and policies in the U.S. oil marketplace, have been misshapen by shale since its start about a decade ago, and headed to a final disaster. I've tried to show how it has managed to disregard normal qualifications for capital and therefore remain a preeminent energy source through a combined cocktail of corporate mismanagement, overenthusiastic capitalization from Wall Street, and a coddling regulatory structure from Washington.

The 'myth' of Saudi America I wrote about in my last book (*Shale Boom, Shale Bust*)—that is, the idea of "American Energy Independence" and its slavish pursuance—has ultimately done tremendous damage to American oil companies, not helped them. Together, we've seen more investor dollars get burned, just as we've seen our sovereign natural resources get burned, with limited benefits to the U.S. economy, investors, or the planet. Negative pricing of oil barrels, even for the moment, is a proof of all that has already been going slowly wrong with U.S. energy. Only now is it, in the face of this global pandemic, showing it at hyperspeed. As the U.S. energy world explodes from coronavirus even more rapidly than other sectors that are impacted more directly by social distancing and negative growth, it is proving that, in the last decade at least, it has always been one of the shakiest sectors of our economy, and most vulnerable to immediate devastation.

For example, when we look at retail—the brick-and-mortar stores like Sears and J.C. Penney and Macy's and Neiman-Marcus—we are quick to understand that online sales have been slowly destroying their model for years and that the bankruptcies we're going to see from coronavirus are merely an accelerant to their inevitable demise. But with U.S. oil, there is a fantasy of necessary survival that remains—for reasons I've talked about—that continues to throw lifelines at them, instead of allowing their bankrupt models to naturally fail as they should. And that has hurt all of us.

And the next stage of the bailout that oil looks likely to get because of the coronavirus could be the biggest ever. Instead of the oil industry finally getting its just desserts from a decade of mismanagement and fraud, the U.S. taxpayer will instead hand it another chance at life that it does not deserve. Many of the efforts the

Federal government has made to combat the economic toll of the coronavirus have been non-specific, to help businesses of all stripes. But because oil companies are in such serious distress, they have been able to access all of these facilities and have participated far more broadly than other sectors. But even more, the Treasury department has expanded the boundaries of those programs particularly for energy companies, making it even easier for them to apply, connect, and receive zero-interest loans and other help.

The first is the small business Payroll Protection Plan loans, a $359 billion program designed to allow small businesses to continue to pay their workers during the shut-downs caused by the pandemic. It was limited to businesses with 500 or fewer employees, and the spirit of the loans was clearly intended for Main-Street-type businesses, such as local restaurants, barber shops, and hardware stores that were forced to close by state-wide shut-downs.

But money for this first round of loans ran out quickly, as businesses of all types applied, including many stripper-well operators and small fracking firms. Even more, the limits on the number of employees for energy companies were expanded by the Treasury department to include far bigger firms: 1,000 employees for gas and oil drilling firms, 1,250 employees for extraction, and 1,250 employees for coal miners.

The PPP wasn't the only specific help to come for distressed oil. In addition, $600b in loans was made available for midsize companies, where the PPP could only accommodate those with a limited number of employees. Here, the threshold for businesses was a payroll with fewer than 10,000 employees and less than $2.5b in revenues—and although that program capped loans at $25 million, oil companies were quick to stand in line for that handout as well.

There's been even more. Treasury Secretary Steve Mnuchin and the Treasury are preparing another $850b in funds to buy bonds of distressed businesses, of which oil companies make up a large minority. Their wide participation is almost written into the outline of the program. The Fed is requiring those assets to have a very low rating in order to participate—BBB-/Baa3 ratings or better, as of March 22—which is an awfully low bar, just marginally above junk status, of which leveraged oil companies bonds comprise another large minority.

But even with these minimal standards to qualify, a consortium of senators from oil states led by Kevin Cramer of North Dakota (Bakken) are leading a charge to push Mnuchin to rate the bonds earlier, in March or February, before Moody's and other bond-ratings services really drop their re-rating boom on oil companies. The timing of this request couldn't be more calculated. On the day that the program was set to be launched, major fracking firm Chesapeake Energy had its bond portfolio downgraded into "C" territory by Moody's, and its stock reacted by dropping more than 20%. (This after its famous 1-for-200 reverse stock split.) If there ever were a program designed to pump life back into the walking dead, this kind of program for already bankrupt companies like Chesapeake seems custom-made.

But there's more. Trump has tweeted his desire to make sure that oil companies don't walk into an early grave, even if their ultimate fate is bankruptcy—at least, not while he's running for reelection.

Donald J. Trump @realDonaldTrump

We will never let the great U.S. Oil & Gas Industry down. I have instructed the Secretary of Energy and Secretary of the Treasury to formulate a plan which will make funds available so that these very important companies and jobs will be secured long into the future!

163K 9:33 AM - Apr 21, 2020

There remains an unallocated fund of about $259b left over from the original $2.6T program that still remains in the Treasury, which Trump might ask to be used directly towards energy companies. There have been rumors (so far, unconfirmed) of a targeted bailout for big oil, with the Democrats getting back previously removed tax incentives for renewables as a 'deal' chip. It seems unlikely that Democrats will take this deal, but Trump remains very interested in keeping U.S. oil—even the weakest companies—alive.

Then there's the possibility of forcing the Texas Commission to halt production through state-wide mandates, or suspending leasehold obligations nationally that force companies to pump oil and gas no matter what the market conditions, or even buying barrels directly for the Strategic Petroleum Reserve in order to try and prop up oil prices temporarily. There are even more options left to this administration, if they really want to ensure that an embattled U.S. energy sector survives.

Much of this is coming down on party lines. While GOP leaders in Washington try to expand the ability of oil companies to participate in these programs and others, they want to exempt them from answering to their many debtors with the funds they get, instead of using them for employee payroll and cash flow. On the other side, Democratic Senator Ed Markey is leading other Democrats in a call to completely exclude the oil and gas industry from all CARES funds designated for coronavirus relief.

I don't know how all of this will turn out (actually, I can pretty safely guess), but I think I've made a case in this book that there is no industrial sector in this country more bloated and less deserving of a bailout using public funds than U.S. Oil, the most likely large-scale recipient of all the many Federal relief programs—and that those continued federal handouts help no one.

Whether you are an investor, an environmentalist, or just a regular taxpayer, you should hate seeing this. It is the culmination of the bad decisions that oil companies, Wall Street, and Washington have made for the past 10 years that has made U.S. oil so much more vulnerable to the economic fallout of a national pandemic than nearly everyone else. Because the oil companies are so vulnerable, they've become the first and most desperately in need of help during the age of coronavirus, even before the airlines and hotels. But their dire need doesn't make them most deserving of it. It's unfair even for investors, who have carefully put money to work in the energy space, correctly steering clear of U.S. independent shale producers who have done nothing but ratchet up debt while continuing to sell more and more oil at a loss. They've instead bought well-run, disciplined energy companies that have pursued conservative drilling and a solid balance sheet, and watched as those investments have soured just as fully as the worst of them. Federal bailouts tend to reward the worst corporate offenders of undisciplined management, while punishing the companies that are in fact the best run. This is antithetical to the 'free market' theories of capital investment, supposedly the bailiwick of Republican and Conservative economists.

Finally, not only does indiscriminate money thrown at bad shale companies invalidate "correct" investment choices of solid energy firms while rewarding the lousy ones. It also puts further into the future the 300-500 restructurings and bankruptcies that are sorely needed to restore the U.S. oil sector into a disciplined and smartly executed group that can, and will, take advantage of the next supply shortage in oil and natural gas that will inevitably come.

Allowing those guys to live will allow them to continue to pump more oil, extend the timeline of low oil prices, and thwart again the natural progression of price and progression towards cleaner energy sources. It shouldn't be allowed to happen.

But I'm guessing it most likely will.

CHAPTER 9:

A CIRCULAR FIRING SQUAD

I've laid out a macroscopic view of the two biggest forces that have been determining oil prices for the last 10 years and currently: OPEC (and mostly by that, I mean Saudi Arabia), and U.S. frackers. It has been the dynamic between these two forces that have mostly determined the rise and (as I'm arguing) destructive fall of oil prices we've seen since 2014, which has sidetracked the 'natural' assimilation of natural gas and ultimately solar and other renewables to gain substantial control of the global energy chain.

We've got to figure out the motivations and strategies of these players during the last 10 years to understand what brought us to the place we're at now and how to navigate going forwards. However, at this point, we also have to bring another very important character into our screenplay about the competition between these two key players and the energy markets: the United States government. Involvement from Washington has always had an impact on global oil and gas markets, but the recent intensity from the Trump administration has turned our mostly one-on-one boxing match into more of a three-way Mexican standoff—or, even more descriptively, a circular firing squad of self-destruction for all.

The United States, and specifically the person occupying the office of the President, has traditionally had a rocky relationship with global oil markets since oil reliance shifted from domestic supplies to international, mostly Arab, supplies in the late 1960s. I'll leave the long history of global oil geopolitics to others, but oil companies had decades of advantageous relationships through the 1970s with foreign governments and their oil resources, backed by the military power of the United States, as well as even more advantageous tax and other incentives back home.

This began to change when foreign countries began to express their sovereignty from the leadership of American-backed monarchs and dictators in the wake of the Vietnam War. In countries like Iran, Iraq, and Saudi Arabia, national oil companies (NOCs) were established with greater independent control in many Middle Eastern oil-producing countries and began to demand more of a share of the profits of their own oil and gas resources from international oil companies. Those 'seven sisters' who dominated global oil and gas from the 1940s through the 1970s (Exxon, Mobil, Chevron, Gulf, Shell, BP, and Texaco) were supplying technology and talent that these less technologically advanced countries needed and couldn't provide for themselves. In exchange for this expertise, the seven sisters were able to 'negotiate' exceedingly advantageous contracts, securing a majority share of the profits from these oil and gas resources, even while tapping extensively in foreign lands.

The first most notable of these rebellions using oil supplies against American interests was exercised by Saudi Arabia during the 1973 oil crisis. The Saudis openly flexed their 'oil' muscles for the first time by boycotting exports to the American markets, a move designed to support their Arab counterparts during the 1973 Arab-Israeli war. This was in response to U.S. support and shipments of armaments to Israel. The boycott was fantastically effective, as it caused a huge shortage—and unprecedented gas-station lines—for U.S. consumers for the first time since the end of gasoline rationing during the Second World War. Americans were not prepared for this inconvenience impacting their daily lives as well as the pressure it caused on the U.S. economy at large, and then President Nixon had a very real problem to deal with: the first real 'rebellion' of an Arab oil state designed to inflict economic harm against the United States. A summit with the Saudis in 1974 ended the boycott, but not before the Saudis gained military support and the favorable relationship with the U.S. that continues to this day.

A second crisis in 1979 again revealed the U.S. vulnerability to Arab oil supplies, as the Iranian revolution deposed the U.S.-backed Shah in favor of an Islamic fundamentalist regime. Iran pushed OPEC to again boycott U.S. markets, but ultimately did not get the agreement of the cartel to go quite that far (the Saudi relationship cemented in 1974 helped in this regard). Still, U.S. supplies were disrupted and gas lines temporarily returned.

These two events were only the start of a series of Middle Eastern geopolitical upheavals that seemed to threaten or genuinely impact the supply of oil to the United States, accompanied often by spiking prices. 1980-81 brought the Iran-Iraq war and further instability to supply and prices. The first Gulf War in 1990 put U.S. troops in the region, ostensibly in defense of Kuwait, but really to support Saudi Arabia and their oil supply against the aggression of Iraq's Saddam Hussein. The result of direct intervention of U.S. forces in the Arab Middle East helped to spike oil prices above $40 a barrel for the first time. The second Gulf War in the shadow of 9/11 drove oil prices to a then-unheard-of $70 a barrel, before collapsing on the day of the U.S. invasion of Iraq.

All of these events, plus dozens of less significant ones, have seemingly convinced every occupant of the White House who followed Nixon and a large component of the U.S. Congress that Middle Eastern supplies of oil to the United States remained consistently under threat, and that one of the responsibilities of the Congress and White House lay in making sure that these supplies remained steady, and their producers in line. Two unspoken but clear policies have been pursued in Washington for the last nearly 50 years designed to 'guarantee' cheap and plentiful oil supplies for the United States consumer.

One was a military dominance in the Middle East with both oil producers and others with influence in oil-producing countries. This U.S.-implied military force was designed to trade domestic security with regimes that maintained cordial relations with the U.S. for help in sustaining U.S. oil streams—and, alternately, to intimidate those regimes that didn't.

Secondly, and more important to our story, it also actively encouraged U.S. oil companies to find and increase domestic oil and gas supplies and reduce exposure to foreign oil sources wherever and whenever possible. The U.S. Congress consistently helped to achieve this by delivering tax incentives for U.S. producers of U.S. oil and gas supplies and by removing regulation at the federal and state levels wherever new sources (whether onshore or offshore) were discovered. The most important side benefit of pursuing domestic supplies instead of trying to enforce the import of foreign ones is obviously the multiple economic benefits of domestic jobs, domestic trade, and domestic pricing.

What I'm describing (in the most admittedly barest form) is the genesis, over decades, of both the obsession in Washington for development of domestic oil supplies and U.S. energy independence from foreign oil. We have heard, particularly in recent years, of the imperative of economic and national security advantages to be gained from a reduced reliance on foreign oil, an idea I tried to debunk in full in my second book, *Shale Boom, Shale Bust: The Myth of Saudi America*. But what's truly important about all of this is to note the combined, apoplectic enthusiasm of both Washington and U.S. oil producers to the prospects of the so-called 'shale revolution' when it first began to take off in the late 2000s.

This short and incomplete history of the United States government and its relationship to fossil fuels for the last 50 years informs several key points about how the White House has approached energy from both OPEC and U.S. producers and where its priorities have been and still, for the most part, remain.

First, it explains the many political benefits of supporting domestic oil companies with various tax advantages and regulatory restraint, both of which benefit the U.S. economy, while pursuing the hope of furthering U.S. energy independence. It also begins to explain many of the complications the U.S. government has had in dealing with both relatively 'friendly' regimes in the Middle East (like the Saudis), as well as with less-friendly regimes (like Iran and Iraq). And perhaps most important, it explains the obsession that many occupants of the White House have had with oil, particularly the price of oil. All presidents have been scared to death of oil shortages and the high prices that naturally follow from them. Gas lines in the '70s proved just how politically tough it could be to occupy the White House during an oil shortage, in a country that has long taken its oil and gasoline supplies for granted. No president to follow Nixon has forgotten the damage that gas lines can do to poll ratings. The bottom line is that White House and Congressional support of U.S. oil producers has had many economic advantages, but equally and often more importantly, political ones.

But no occupant of the White House has been as obsessed with the unencumbered flow of oil from the Middle East as well as the success of U.S. oil producers as the U.S. administration of Donald Trump, whose influence on oil prices have been more immediate and consequential than any other President perhaps in history.

Because of Trump's efforts at influencing oil supply and oil prices, what we've been experiencing in the oil markets since 2016 hasn't been the oft-referred "mano-a-mano" standoff between U.S. oil companies and OPEC that's been most often represented in the media—that is, a battle between the two over market share and prices. Instead, President Trump has particularly turned those battles into more of a three-way Mexican standoff, with all three participants standing in a circle with guns loaded and threatening to blaze away without any control over who they're shooting at. The conflicting needs of the President to promote economic success for U.S. companies, while trying to ensure foreign oil supplies remain robust, all while trying to keep oil prices low have not only been contradictory, but frankly impossible. The resulting signals Trump has given to U.S. energy companies and conflicting others to the Saudis have had nothing but destructive outcomes for energy markets. And as with any circular firing squad, so far, no one has come out unscathed. Everyone's been a loser, with both OPEC and U.S. frackers teetering on the edge of disaster.

Let's take a deeper dive into all three of our players: Our two primary modern combatants in our global oil war— OPEC and U.S. frackers—really shouldn't be at all at odds with each other. After all, both the Saudis and U.S. oil companies have the same clear goal in mind: to see oil prices as high as possible. I've already noted OPEC's (and particularly the Saudis') desperate need for higher oil prices. I've also noted how much U.S. oil producers have banked their survival on higher oil prices, but are yet 'forced' into increasing production and constantly adding to the global surplus, short-circuiting this goal. Even with this roadblock, the desperate need for expensive oil by both should at some point, we'd guess, find its way to equilibrium, especially as fracking has continued to mature.

Indeed, it has been a fundamental contention of mine since 2014 that as U.S. fracking continued out of its infancy, it would have to gravitate naturally towards that equilibrium. Like the classic example of DeBeers and its pricing of diamonds, the frackers' "higher goal" of encouraging $100 oil would sink in, and they'd apply the proper discipline in spending and production to achieve that, helping themselves as well as their competition, OPEC and the Saudis. Instead, we've seen these bad habits die very hard indeed—and before any single oil company has been willing to unilaterally slash its spending and output, it has been far more willing to point at the next U.S. producer instead and say, "you first."

I'm going to talk a lot more about possible solutions to this behavior in Chapter 11, which could help to get U.S. producers on the same page with OPEC+ producers. But since 2010, I've made clear in previous sections how U.S. oil companies have been consistently putting pressure on markets instead with rising production irrespective of price, short-circuiting the natural alliance they have with the Saudis to promote higher prices.

SAUDI ARABIA (AND OPEC)

For the Saudis, much of their response to this has been more reactionary than retaliatory. U.S. production increases have forced the Saudis also into admittedly self-defeating behavior, flooding the global markets and creating a subsequent lethal price war with U.S. frackers. Since 2014, this has happened not once, not twice, but three times in the last six years. Since we're trying to find a way to get oil prices higher and keep them there, it would be good to explore why the Saudis are continually short-circuiting the markets themselves while destroying their own profits simultaneously.

The first episode in 2014 was a calculated policy turn designed to combat U.S. shale production gains head-on. When it became clear through unchecked increases from 2011-2014 that U.S. frackers were unwilling (or incapable) of controlling production, the Saudi king changed strategy from negotiated quotas in the cartel to directly addressing this new competition in the United States for the first time. He was following the advice of his long-time oil minister Ali Al-Naimi, who saw no alternative but to attack U.S. producers with rock-bottom prices. In late 2014, the Saudis announced and subsequently flooded the markets with barrels, causing the first tremendous price collapse, moving oil prices from well over $100 to finally bottom under $30 a barrel in early 2016, as you can see in Figure 9.1.

Figure 9.1.
The Three "Rounds" of the Oil Price Collapse (2014-2020)

But this death match initiated by Saudi Arabia did not have nearly the result it sought, and it did not drive many of the major U.S. fracking interests out of business. Although 500 small U.S. oil companies succumbed to these lower prices, the larger-cap and larger-producing shale players who were the primary targets continued to survive. We've explored how they managed to hang on, in Chapter 3 on shale oil, through support from both Washington and Wall Street. But when this two-year pressure on oil prices failed to deliver the death blow to U.S. frackers that was intended, the Saudis, facing their own increasing financial risks from low oil prices, changed policy again.

In a tremendous upheaval that consolidated young Prince Mohammed bin Salman's power in the Kingdom, Al-Naimi and several other high-ranking officials in the Saudi government were removed and replaced. The new oil minister, Khalid Al-Falih, was charged with a startling new plan: not only to reinstate deep production cuts within OPEC to rebalance the oil markets, but also to begin a new partnership in those production cuts between OPEC and Russia. Al-Falih and MbS amazingly secured this deal, cutting an unprecedented 2 million barrels a day cut between the two oil behemoths.

So we can say that Round One of this death match between OPEC and U.S. frackers, which lasted from the end of 2014 to the start of 2016, went to...well, no one. OPEC was forced to abandon its price war without fully getting its desired result, and U.S. oil companies swooned in the wake of low oil prices, taking down more investor money, going further in debt or, if they were smaller, bought by other firms or forced into bankruptcy court. If they were lucky enough to avoid restructuring, they did it by digging themselves a deeper hole of debt, and consequently becoming ever more desperate for cash flow.

The new OPEC+ deal at the start of 2016 created the enormous price rebound in oil. The alliance between Saudi Arabia and Russia proved to be very effective, slowly but surely working to empty the enormous gluts that years of oversupply from both U.S. and OPEC producers had created, and prices slowly began to recover. Continued negotiated production cuts from OPEC+ from 2016 until 2018 brought prices back to close to $80 in late Fall of 2018.

Then, unexpectedly and seemingly out of the blue, Saudi Arabia again signaled that all quotas were "off" and OPEC members were free to "open their spigots." Such a strange unilateral change from a spectacularly successful policy of cuts created through delicate negotiations with Russia was presented by the Saudis again as a response to rampant U.S. production. And while it was certainly true that U.S. production was taking full advantage of higher prices and rapidly increasing production, this explanation was not entirely believable. The Saudi history of oil policy overhauls had historically been accompanied by very careful preparation and clear prior signals. Instead, it seemed more than circumstantial that this announcement also came on the heels of Secretary of State Pompeo's visit to Riyadh to discuss the Khashoggi killing, as I speculated in Chapter 4.

In hindsight, it has also become clear that another incentive for the Saudis to suddenly increase production and force prices downwards (in front of the 2018 midterm elections) was not only to get a pass from the U.S. on the murder of the journalist, but also an undisclosed and Congressionally unauthorized arms sales agreement with the Kingdom. This quiet deal, which the White House used "emergency" measures to implement without Congress, was being investigated by the State Department Inspector General, Steve Linick, when he was summarily dismissed from his job in May of 2020.

In all cases, this Round Two of the price war began on the heels of that announcement, dropping prices quickly towards $40. It destroyed the delicate relationship that had been slowly cultivated between the Saudis and the Russians over the previous two years, and it paved the way for the suspicion between the two that emerged during the coronavirus outbreak. Meanwhile, this flooding of the markets and consequent fast drop in prices had only one apparent winner: Trump.

I've examined Round Three of these recurring price wars extensively, in Chapters 7 and 8 on the reaction to the coronavirus in the Spring of 2020. The winners in this round have been decidedly hard to find again, and certainly not either the Saudis or the Russians. Even this massive drop of prices down below $20 a barrel (and even negative (!) prices for a few strange hours) didn't help President Trump, who suddenly had no use for such low oil prices, not when they were so low as to threaten the entire U.S. oil sector. (As Trump's tweet in Chapter 8 shows.)

The point is that low oil prices during this critical period have benefited no-one—arguably not even the American consumer—while injuring the long-term plans of the Saudis to recapitalize their country, the Russians to stabilize their market share, or the American shale players, whom we turn back to now.

How were U.S. producers faring through these three price wars, all initiated by OPEC?

U.S. SHALE PRODUCERS FEEL THE PAIN OF THE PRICE BUST

Throughout this book, I've noted the inexorable increase of supply of oil and gas from shale from U.S. producers from 2010 onwards. And through this critical period between 2014 and 2020 when the coronavirus hit, no "traditional" market forces seemed to be able to detour this behavior. I've shown the charts for U.S. production elsewhere, but let's take a look at another chart describing U.S. oil production: the rig counts in Figure 9.2.

Figure 9.2.
U.S. Oil Drill Rigs (1990-2020)

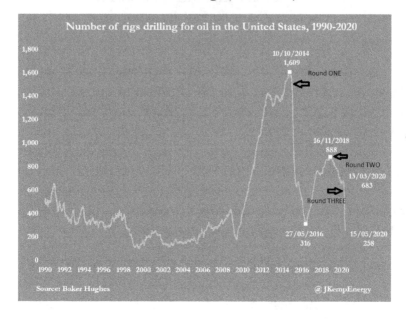

It's immediately clear from Figure 9.2 that U.S. oil producers are not nuanced when it comes to putting new rigs to work drilling for oil: since 2010, they've either been at full speed or full contraction. Since 2010, when the enthusiasm of fracking revived an oil and gas industry laid to waste by the 2007 economic crisis, oil rigs skyrocketed, until the OPEC announcement of what I'm calling Round One of the three-round market-share war that began in 2014.

If we could superimpose (in our minds) the price of oil and U.S. production onto the chart in Figure 9.2 of U.S. drilling interest (with Figure 3.3, for example), we'd see some very obvious and interesting patterns. First, we would see how strongly the spike of oil prices above $80 and even above $100 a barrel coincided with the intense ramping up of drilled rigs and U.S. production from the years 2010- 2104. This makes total sense. With oil prices high, there was little reason for anyone in the U.S. oil business not to move full speed ahead with drilling. Almost every shale project in the United States could boast a positive re-turn at triple-digit oil prices. But this enthusiasm, combined both with the belief that oil would never price below $100 a bar-rel and the prime directive of all oil companies to continually grow, spurred shale E&Ps to ever-greater production commit-ments. Vast spending increases as well as production increases meant that U.S. shale producers needed to utilize all forms of public and private capital and debt, in order to continually add rigs and increase output. But it also meant that oil companies were becoming more and more vulnerable to any kind of price disruption, and that a price collapse below profitable levels—or breakevens—could be catastrophic.

Now look at what happened to rigs as oil hit the skids through the Saudi and OPEC efforts to crater prices in 2014. Companies cut back on new rigs and slowed completion of existing drilling (and created a new glut of drilled but uncompleted (DUC) wells).

But while the cuts in completed wells through the erosion of spent assets combined with the conversion of ongoing projects into DUCs did a marvelous job of dropping rig counts and curb-ing spending somewhat, it did shockingly little to slow the U.S. output of oil. If we refer again to Figure 3.3 (or 2.2), we see that oil production only dropped a million barrels a day in the two years of that first bust I wrote so extensively about in 2015. This is in contrast to the massive oil boom where producers added to the global supply in the previous four years—an incredible four million barrels a day between 2010 and 2014.

How did the U.S. manage to retain so much oil production while the number of rigs were dropping so spectacularly? We've already noted in Chapter 6 on shale that this two-year period saw amazing efficiency gains in spacing and fracking technology, which allowed producers to deliver nearly as much oil and gas to markets while still curtailing rigs by more than 80%. We could give credit to the ingenious ability of most large-cap oil companies to survive this Round-One price war—and many of the oil companies at the conventions I attended at the time were fast to do so themselves. I remember one where the motto for the entire gathering, printed on hats and t-shirts, was "Keep Calm and Frack On."

But despite the resourcefulness of U.S. oil to withstand the market share war that Saudi Arabia began in 2014, those nearly two years dug very deep holes for the U.S. oil industry and dictated their response going forwards. The first relief came when OPEC+ was born and returned production discipline to the global marketplace, cutting nearly 2 million barrels a day and setting a price target of $60 a barrel. It was during this next period that U.S. producers took full advantage of the "cover" that the new OPEC+ alliance was giving the global markets. Hungry for cash flow to feed the capital requirements that had seen them through the 2014 bust, oil producers didn't waste a moment to turn up their output as high and as fast as it would go, using all the efficiency gains they had learned to drill and pump oil at a record pace. This was all despite the fact that oil prices never went much above $65 a barrel, or ever threatened to return to the golden profits of triple-digit oil. In fact, it became clear that the breakneck production gains in the U.S. were the reason the markets never saw these now-lofty numbers. From the middle of 2016 through the next "flood" of crude that was unleashed by Saudi Arabia in the fall of 2018, rigs increased nearly three-fold, and U.S. production increased an astounding 5 million plus (!) barrels a day.

This critical moment in the history of U.S. fracking is made exceedingly clear using this rig-count chart in Figure 9.2, over all others. Take a look again at the movement of rigs during this 2016-2018 period against the production growth chart of Figure 3.3. We can see that the increase in the number of actual platforms producing oil went up, but it never came anywhere close to seeing the number they saw at their peak in 2014; in fact, they were 50% lower.

But despite this, production not only exceeded what was accomplished in 2014, it exceeded it by nearly 4 million barrels a day. And all this was accomplished even though those barrels were only marginally profitable at the end of this cycle, and not for the majority of the time before.

At this point, I should make clear again that the lack of discipline in spending and production that's been shown from oil producers during this crucial period from 2016 to the fall of 2018 isn't entirely their own fault. Wall Street (both the analysts and investors there) had until only very recently valued increased production—over everything else—from U.S. E&Ps as the singular "golden grail" metric in assessing relative success. Therefore, this has been another incentive for oil companies to pursue continue production increases as the one overwhelming quarterly and yearly goal—both from the smallest 10-barrel-a-day fracker to the largest mega-cap major.

But it's important to emphasize again how independent frackers have particularly pursued this lone metric without regards to much else. And it's here that Wall Street shares a healthy portion of the blame for this behavior. Only through the realization of increased production, year after year, have oil producers managed to keep their credit ratings relatively high and attract favorable recommendations—which then helps to drive higher stock prices through the investment appetites of funds, private equity, and individual investors. If you wanted to keep yourself vibrant in the oil patch, oil executives in both large and particularly small energy companies have needed to prove growth at all costs in order to keep investment capital flowing in.

Some oil companies who might have wished for a more balanced approach to valuing their efforts have in fact voiced their concern...at times. Some, on rare occasions, have complained loudly about this singular metric as the only one that mattered to investors. CEO Al Walker of Anadarko Petroleum (before its buy-out by Occidental) was particularly vocal about Wall Street's lack of focus on investor returns on capital. I note these complaints with interest but also with a certain skepticism, as most executive bonuses have been equally tethered to increasing production as well.

Meanwhile, it was during this run-up to Round Two of the circular firing squad that oil companies who had managed to survive the attempted Saudi purge in 2014 managed to put themselves at even greater risk for a downturn in oil prices. And when it came in the Fall of 2018, when Saudi producers opened the spigots again, independent U.S. E&Ps lost the last of whatever enthusiasm was left for shale production and became one of the least investable sectors in the economy. The game was essentially over.

TRUMP AND THE UNITED STATES GOVERNMENT

It's here we must again circle back to the U.S. government and President Trump as an equally insidious force as Wall Street analysts and bond rating agencies, hurting both U.S. oil companies and OPEC from pursuing their mutual goals of high oil prices.

This is precisely because Trump's goals have been so inconsistent. On the one hand, the President has shown an obsessive political desire to maintain low oil prices; on the other, an economic need to support U.S. energy companies and their profits. On every occasion when these dual incongruent goals have been applied, both OPEC *and* U.S. energy companies have come away as losers. With these competing goals in play, it has been impossible for any President to really be a useful ally in our need to get oil prices higher. But with President Trump and his overwhelmingly strong applications of force in every direction, that roadblock has become almost insurmountable.

Trump's dual desires on oil are not unique. We know that Trump is not the first president to have acted to keep oil prices low. George Bush visited the Saudi King in early 2008, only months before the onset of the financial crisis, begging for more oil supplies from Saudi Arabia and OPEC: he was trying to turn the tide on an oil price that had become overheated, streaking towards a high of $147 a barrel. The collapse in all financial markets later that year did the job far better than the Saudis could have, even if they wanted to help the U.S. President, which they most certainly did not. Still, surely a global financial collapse was not the answer that Bush had in mind.

Bush wasn't alone in his attempts to keep a lid on oil prices for political reasons, either. Bill Clinton released oil from the SPR in front of the 2000 elections in a bid to help his Vice-President Al Gore. President Obama also released oil from the Strategic Reserve in 2011 during the Libya crisis. The widespread theory, held by many economists and certainly believed by many presidents, is that high oil prices, besides making voters angry, also leads to a recession, a political disaster for incumbents – note the relative gas prices for the last three U.S. administrations, as shown in Figure 9.3.

Figure 9.3.
A Snapshot of Gas Prices for the Last Three U.S. Administrations

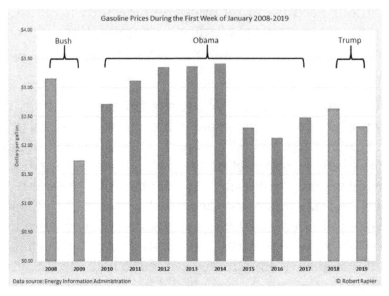

Trump has certainly taken that lesson to heart, more than any other president to date. Also, he has arguably had far more impact on oil prices in the short term than any other president in history as well. The most notable effect was in late 2018, when Trump "made a deal" with the Saudis to increase production at a time when they least wanted to. I've already speculated that this deal was related to the Khashoggi killing, but whether it was or not, it clearly added further supply into an oil market that was just beginning to clear the gluts from the previous three years. And in terms of the goals of the other two participants of our circular firing squad, it benefited neither: both the Saudis and Prince MbS were forced to delay their Saudi Aramco IPO again, and their hopes for Vision 2030 and U.S. frackers have had to bear exceedingly depressed oil prices since.

Since that first meddling with global oil markets, Trump has engaged throughout his first term in several other tweets, messages, and outright threats to try and continue to bully the Saudis into raising production for the benefit of U.S. producers and to maintain low oil prices at home. Throughout this period, he has also aggressively used his Energy, Transportation, and Interior departments as well as the Environmental Protection Agency to relieve regulatory restraints on the oil and gas industry, further encouraging oil companies to overproduce. While the Interior department has relaxed restrictions for drilling on U.S. wetlands and withdrew justification to restrain mercury emissions from power plants, most of the so-called help for energy companies has come through the EPA. In total, the EPA has reversed 100 environmental rules and regulations in place to control carbon, and most of the major climate advances put into place by the previous Obama administration, including previous limits on automobile emissions, fracking wastewater, methane exhaust, fracking chemicals, drilling in the Arctic, a weakened review of pipeline permits, and dozens of others.

Whether you are outraged by the rollbacks of environmental guidelines (which have pushed U.S. climate policy back towards the 1970s), or whether you feel that regulation under President Obama had reached unnecessary levels and needed restraint, the end result of this effort encouraged continued misappropriation of capital and energy resources by U.S. oil and gas independents—and unfettered overproduction into unprofitable markets.

I made another study of Trump's moves during the coronavirus pandemic in Chapters 7 and 8, when he was forced ultimately to reverse his traditional goals of lower oil prices when those prices nearing zero threatened the entirety of the sector's survival. In addition, we saw the extensive financial support that was given by the CARES act and the backstop of Treasury asset purchases. This Round-Three outcome, as a result of the Trump administration's reactions to the pandemic, is yet to be fully seen, but from all indications there will again be no winners: Trump's hopes of a quick rebound for the U.S. economy look to be impossible, particularly in the oil and gas sector, despite all the many helping hands that have been extended. (Update: despite the stock market indexes seeing new highs in 2020, oil sector stocks remain depressed.)

In fact, we have seen that the outcomes from all three "rounds" of the energy market price wars that have occurred in the last six years have been nothing but horrible for everyone involved. No one—not the Saudis, U.S. oil companies, or President Trump—have gotten entirely what they wanted. Even the Russians, who had sacrificed for two years their own goals of production increases to help OPEC keep prices elevated have seen these efforts fail, as well as incite two price wars with their temporary cartel partners. As for the Saudis, they have been unable to destroy their U.S. competition, despite twice flooding the markets and annihilating prices. U.S. oil companies have been unable to control their production no matter how many clues of inevitable ruin that the market gave them. Oil prices continued to languish well under any margin of reasonable return on their production, they sank further and further into debt and the pressure of endless new capital requirements and their shares have seen nothing but lower, and ever-sinking prices. Finally, even President Trump has been forced to move alternately between policies that promote lower oil prices to those that backstop U.S. energy companies from the ill effects of lower oil prices.

In all ways, a laughable circular firing squad of misdirected effort from all.

CHAPTER 10:

NATURAL GAS: THAT PRETTIEST, BUT STILL IGNORED, GIRL IN ALL THOSE MOVIES

There's a very good reason why I've left the chapter on natural gas, supposedly our next step along the evolutionary energy train, until late in this book. Any discussion of natural gas cannot be started without having at least a general understanding of crude oil first. It's never been the other way around. You can talk all you want about oil (and the financial media does it exclusively all the time) without mentioning natural gas once. In contrast, natural gas is often only referred to by natural gas "specialists," whereas you'll see just about anyone, without the slightest credentials, confidently offer up their opinion on crude oil.

Why is that?

Drilled wells almost always yield a combination of natural gas and oil. I'm going to talk about the relative amounts of gas and oil that are coming out of the ground here in the United States, because that's also critically important for understanding the natural gas (and the shale oil) markets.

What we first need to understand when talking about natural gas is how that relative yield of oil and gas is a key element of the entire fossil fuel production chain. Natural gas, except for those energy companies that are "lucky" enough to have a very, very low relative percentage of gas to oil, must take the markets for natural gas into consideration as they will impact their exploration and production plans and marketing behavior.

Why is that? Well, simply because although both oil and natural gas are fossil fuels, they trade far differently and are rarely worth the same to oil companies. And when I say the same, let's be simple and quantify both in terms of their energy yield in Btus (British Thermal Units). It doesn't exactly turn the comparison of oil and natural gas from apples and oranges into apples and apples, but it is the best way to come close.

Oil is priced everywhere in barrels, with a barrel of oil containing 42 gallons. Natural gas is priced in cubic feet and more often in millions of cubic feet (Mmcf). When we are pricing natural gas, we often jump a step and refer directly to the Btus released by burning a cubic foot of natural gas. A British Thermal Unit is defined as the amount of energy needed to raise a pound of water one degree Fahrenheit; it is a direct measure of energy. By very good fortune, we are lucky that a cubic foot of natural gas will deliver 1.025 Btu—and in the real world, almost everyone forgets this negligible difference and equates the two values. So, it doesn't matter if we're talking about an Mmcf (1 million cubic feet) or an MmBtu (1 million Btus) of natural gas, it is, at least in practice, the same amount.

Now to find equivalence. A barrel of oil has 5.8 MmBtu of potential energy. From this simple conversion, we can get to a very famous statistic used by energy companies the world over: the barrel of oil-equivalent (BOE). For oil and gas companies, they often quote their reserves (that is, the total amount of oil and gas that they have control over and can drill for) and their production (the amount they actually bring out of the ground), using this shorthand of barrels of oil equivalent (BOEs), lumping both oil and gas together by potential energy and making them a single number.

It seems like a good idea, simplifying oil and gas as the same thing, right? After all, they're both fossil fuels and burn, don't they? Yes, although they both burn; no, they're not quite the same thing, and often the BOE numbers hide what oil companies are trying not to say out loud—which is their definite preference for one over the other.

For example, if you are an energy company and you write up in your quarterly report how you produced 1000 BOEs, no one can tell from that lone number how much of that is oil and how much is gas. Sure, you can find the absolute amount of both if you search deeper in the report but almost always it is oil and not gas that energy companies prefer, and they'd like their gas reserves to be quantified 'as if' they were just as good. For them, it's great to refer to natural gas using an "equivalent" measure to oil, even though it's not. I'll explain why energy companies often prefer oil over natural gas, later in the chapter.

A BRIEF HISTORY OF NATURAL GAS

But first, let's have a quick (and I mean quick) history lesson about natural gas, and the many characteristics that make it very different from oil. Natural gas occurs in the real world in the same way that crude oil does. As an "associated" component of an oil well, it is similarly trapped under the ground or deep in the ocean, and it is released when an opening is created where it can escape under either its own or applied pressure. So, we'll chalk up one important and major similarity between oil and gas: you drill and you get both to come out of the same well.

Yet, in the early days of the development of fossil fuels and despite often coming out of the same well, oil was given tremendous preference over natural gas. Why? Because it was a far easier resource to make immediate use of, as it emerged from the ground in liquid form. In the early decades of the 20th century, liquid oil proved easier to capture, transport, and manipulate into several different refined products for varying needs. Natural gas was more difficult to capture, control, and transport and required pipelines and storage tanks at every locus where it was moved, recollected, and finally used. Besides some jobs in lighting and heating, natural gas found few other immediate uses and none where oil couldn't (and wasn't) often substituted for it.

Remember, these were times when there was no concern about the limited resources or prices of either oil or gas; there was merely an issue of which was easier to get out of the ground and to the places where it would be most usefully burned. For this reason, natural gas became the far-less-developed component of well drilling—a second sister—always running behind the infrastructure spending and networks that oil and its refined products enjoyed.

It hasn't been so one-sided for quite a long time, but still, the investment over nearly a century "biased" towards oil continues today, with few producers and end users happily willing to see those investments adjusted or scrapped for environmental benefits alone. In all ways, while natural gas has languished as the obvious alternative to oil, oil products have continued to dominate. "Natty's" long history of being the ignored sister of oil well production, as well as a lack of a national policy to help move it forwards, has kept natural-gas advocates at a serious disadvantage over the decades, and particularly the most important last two decades.

Further, as well as laboring against this disadvantaged market placement, natural gas has still often been unfairly lumped together with oil as just another "fossil fuel"—burdened with an equal share of the environmental negatives it didn't deserve while getting little credit it has deserved as a viable, full-service energy source.

But let's examine some of the many reasons why that's just wrong and why we must, finally, throw off this archaic approach to natural gas.

THE ADVANTAGES OF NATURAL GAS VS. OIL

First, let's look at the relative values of oil versus natural gas. A barrel of oil generates 5.8 times more energy than an Mmcf of natural gas. Natural gas is always priced per Million Btus—and that price has varied over the past 15 years in a very wide range, but in the past 10 years and certainly since the economic crisis of 2008, it has stayed mostly between $1.50 and $4.00 per MmBtu, as you can see in Figure 10.1.

Figure 10.1.
Natural Gas Prices (2009-2020)

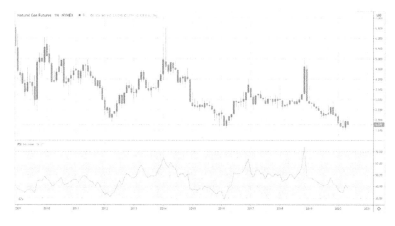

In order to calculate an equivalence of cost for an equivalence of energy of both sources, we can multiply the cost of natural gas by 5.8 (it takes that much to equal a barrel of oil) and compare, which gives us an "equivalent energy" cost of natural gas between $8.70 and $23.20 for an equivalent barrel of oil, at least in the recent markets of the past 10 years. That's a pretty cheap barrel of oil (equivalent energy potential), when we've become accustomed to oil ranging often closer to $100, at least in the decade from 2003 through 2014.

Figure 10.2 charts both natural gas and oil prices concurrently, with the price for natural gas represented by the right Y-axis and the line associated to it, and oil represented by the left Y-axis and the line associated to it. It attempts to make the energy conversion we speak of in the previous paragraph and chart them so that their 'relative' prices are represented equally. In actuality, however, if Figure 10.2 were measured solely by Btu equivalence, natural gas would be skewed even lower, with greater advantage than it's being shown here—with, for example, a $4/mmBtu natural gas price equating to a $23.20/barrel price for oil as we've said, and not the near $40 price represented here.

Nevertheless, Figure 10.2 does as good job as I can find representing the tremendous change in the natural gas market since the financial crisis of 2008 and the beginning of the U.S. natural gas fracking boom soon after. Before widespread fracking, natural gas prices ranged far higher, often spiking north of $6 and even $8 an MmBtu – in many cases, being worth as much, if not more than crude oil. In many countries where shale fracking doesn't exist, such as Europe and Japan, it still does see these relatively high prices regularly. But here in the U.S., the incredible success of gas fracking since the late 2000s has dropped the cost of natural gas fantastically far below the equivalent cost of oil. Even looking at this chart that we know has already optimistically skewed natural gas prices upward compared to oil by $15 an equivalent barrel, we still see the relative prices of natural gas lag far behind those of oil since the recovery from the financial crisis of 2008. And it seems, from all indications, that it is likely to stay that way for many years, likely even decades to come. Chalk up one advantage for natural gas over oil: It's cheaper, and likely to stay that way.

Figure 10.2.
Relative prices of Oil (left Y-axis) vs. Natural Gas (right Y-axis)
(1995-2020)

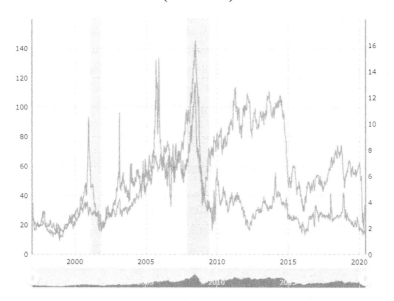

Early in this book, I made a case that the resources for fracked oil are quickly running dry, and that the likely boom in production for oil fracking is fast coming to a close, even with production numbers that currently race higher. However, the numbers for natural gas fracking are grossly different, and they indicate that our supply will truly last for decades, with 500 trillion cubic feet of proven reserves and another 2500 trillion cubic feet of unproven reserves on tap here in the United States, according to the EIA. At the current domestic demand of about 30 trillion cubic feet a year, our reserves should supply us comfortably for the next 90 years. Even if we managed to move more positively towards natural gas use and perhaps even push it towards three times its current demand (unlikely at best), we'd still have reserves—that is, completely domestic (energy-independent!) supplies—that would easily last through 2050. Chalk up advantage number two: We've got lots of gas, and it's not quickly running out, like oil.

More positive news for natural gas: While I've made the equivalency (as most of the energy world does) between oil and natural gas based on the amount of energy released for each as you burn it, I haven't taken into account the amount of energy needed to turn crude oil into something practical you can actually burn. Remember, crude oil is worthless by itself: it is only through the refining of it into usable products that it has practical energy value as gasoline and diesel fuel and heating oil and jet fuel etc. The average refinery uses 8.4 kilowatt hours to refine a barrel of oil, which at an average price of electricity in the United States equates to an added $1.25 per barrel, a significant added cost. You also obviously need to build a refinery, staff it, pay salaries, buy insurance, and guard against fires and other disasters—which are all costs that natural gas doesn't have.

Now, some advocates for heating oil will say that an equivalent amount of oil will burn slower and hotter than natural gas, making all approach equality again—to which I say, probably not. Even if you believe the hype of the American Energy Coalition (the national organization of heating oil producers and suppliers), natural gas has the advantage of being in final form for use as it emerges from the wellhead that no refined product can beat. There are no storage or refining costs; with our modern extensive roadmap of pipelines, all you need to do is point it straight from the well to where it's needed, and you're in business.

In terms of environmental advantages, natural gas is also far, far advanced, certainly to coal for power plants, where it is twice as "clean," emitting half the amount of carbon, but also to any grade of crude oil in the world, even the cleanest burning "sweet" crudes. According to the EIA, natural gas emits 117 pounds of CO_2 per MmBtu burned, whereas refined heating oil emits 161 pounds, an improvement of 27%. Environmentalists will claim that all the improvements in carbon emissions for natural gas are mitigated by the methane leaks that are endemic to natural gas drilling, but these can be easily addressed with more stringent national regulation and oversight, which I'll discuss in Chapter 11— when I suggest possible energy plans that move natural gas further up the energy chain. For now, let's agree on the obvious: natural gas is a step forwards environmentally from crude oil and certainly a major improvement for electricity generation over coal.

It's cheaper, more abundant, and cleaner. But the advantages for natural gas don't end there.

Natural gas is particularly different from oil in that it cannot be globally priced. This makes natural gas markets entirely different than crude oil markets, which have the same prices everywhere. But natural gas cannot be one universal price worldwide simply because it's so difficult to transport. The most common way that natural gas is transported is through pipelines, and you can't practically put pipelines that cross seas. You can transport natural gas from one continent to another if you transform it into a liquid, by cooling it to extreme temperatures (-260F) and storing it in containers that can maintain such temperatures—a form know as Liquid Natural Gas (LNG), which I discussed briefly in the preface. This business of cooling and storing natural gas so it can be transported from one place to another without pipelines continues to gain in activity and represents an important part of local natural gas markets in major exporters like Qatar and Australia. But here in the United States, although it is gaining in importance, it is still not yet truly significant or impacting the natural gas markets much. And it's expensive as well, costing anywhere from \$2 to \$4 per Mmcf extra to convert and then transport to another foreign market.

Most important, because natural gas resists traditional and far cheaper modes of transport, it is also a necessarily more local market than oil. In other words, every network of pipelines for natural gas will create its own unique prices based on its very local supply and demand, since you cannot easily move an excess of gas to a place where there is a shortage, as you can in so many ways with oil. Prices for natural gas, therefore, vary wildly from Japan to Eastern Europe, Australia, Indonesia, Great Britain, and the United States. To be precise, there are some variants in the prices for various crudes around the world where they are produced as well, but compared to natural gas, those prices represent simple differences in grades and the known, fixed costs for traditional tanker or other overland transport. In natural gas, because transport between countries and their distinct markets is expensive and sometimes impossible, each market's pricing remains essentially independent. Local prices for gas in every individual network will depend on how strong the local supply chain and localized demand are. To use two gross examples, in Europe and Japan, where there is very little local production of natural gas, prices are much higher, while in Russia and the United States, where local production is huge (and often is far greater than the local demand), prices are much, much cheaper.

Practically speaking, and this is the most important distinction, we can say that oil is a GLOBAL market, while natural gas is a LOCAL one. That means, crucially, that when something affects the supply or demand for oil anywhere in the world, all prices for oil are equally affected everywhere, whereas it takes a local change in supply or demand of natural gas to effect a change of price in its respective local market, leaving prices everywhere else for the most part untouched.

Immediately upon knowing that natural gas is, for all intents and purposes, a localized market, you can see the many further advantages that it could have here in the U.S. over oil. Since its local prices are unaffected by foreign geopolitics, it doesn't matter what happens in the Middle East; whether a war is breaking out, or if an Arab nation decides to boycott exports to the U.S., or any other disruption. In all cases, local U.S. natural gas prices will remain essentially the same. Since U.S. natural gas supplies are abundant, the idea of true energy independence becomes a real possibility and not merely political rhetoric. There is no longer any need to effect national energy policy to apply pressures to maintain supplies from foreign oil producers, nor is there a need to create a regulatory framework or incentives for domestic natural gas drilling, with the primary goal to offset foreign production, as there is with oil production here at home. Whatever natural gas you can drill for at home is ready to be bought, sold, and used, here at home.

The "early days" of fossil fuel extraction and development favored crude oil because of its ease of transport as a liquid and the many usable forms of its refined products: gasoline for cars, diesel fuel for trucks, heating oil for home and factory boilers, jet fuel for airlines. But today, it can be argued that natural gas wins every direct battle with oil. It emerges from the wellhead in one form and can be transported wherever pipelines are available, which today is virtually everywhere. It can be converted using modern technology into almost any crude oil refined product (e.g., gasoline, diesel, jet fuel) for an average cost of approximately $1 a gallon, making even those converted products far cheaper than "regular" refined products over the last nearly 12 years. And, of course, it can be used more efficiently without any kind of conversion at all in cars and buses and trucks: everyone has seen various city vehicles sporting the "CNG" logo (which stands for *compressed natural gas*). Conversions for trucks from gasoline to CNG vehicles using an added pressurized tank in a trunk or truck bed have long been available. Even for small consumer cars, a natural gas alternative has been commercially available for decades: Honda has made a natural-gas-powered Civic for consumer purchase for more than 20 years. However, all of these offerings have failed to capture a significant portion of the market.

At this point, you'd be right to ask, *What, are we nuts? Why haven't we moved as a country towards natural gas as our primary fuel and abandoned crude oil?*

WHY OIL IS STILL WINNING INSTEAD OF NATURAL GAS

The truth is that natural gas has continued to grow its share (see Fig. 2-4), just not nearly as spectacularly as this long list of advantages would suggest. And some of the answer to why that is the case lies in the early development of crude oil infrastructure I discussed earlier and the lack of vision and aggressive incentives for natural gas from Washington. But the most important reason comes from big consolidated oil companies that drill and produce both oil and natural gas, and one you can probably guess at: *Money.* For oil and gas companies, oil has been far more profitable than natural gas to produce for most of the last 30 years, except for a few brief moments in the 2000s. The discovery and widespread use of shale drilling was originally intended to help augment the production of natural gas. In the early days of fracking, it was thought that the stimulation between shale layers by fracking fluids under pressure was only useful in getting gasses to flow more readily, and not liquids. It was only nearly a decade later that these techniques were refined for use to stimulate new oil and natural gas liquids (NGLs) to flow in oil-rich shale areas in the Dakotas and Texas.

Early fracking efforts focused in areas of the United States that delivered overwhelming ratios of natural gas compared to oil: in Oklahoma, Louisiana, Ohio, New York, and Pennsylvania. Early fracking for natural gas in these areas proved not only to yield easy and cheap gas, but spurred a "gold rush" towards ever-larger shale plays and seemingly endless new sources. The boom in leasing, fracking, and production in the Haynesville, Barnett, Antrim, and the Marcellus also had another predictable effect (that somehow escaped its producers): It cratered prices. Starting in late 2007, U.S. natural gas collapsed from nearly $12/mMBtu to under $4 from the overwhelming excess that the natural gas fracking boom in the early 2000s created, an excess from which prices have still not recovered.

As both natural gas and oil began to yield to fracking as a new source of production, those energy companies that had the resources to focus on one more than the other, not surprisingly, chose to concentrate on oil, where global markets kept prices for oil far higher than the domestic markets, with its continual excess, did for natural gas. Higher global prices simply translate into higher profits. This is what makes the ratio of oil to gas of any particular fracking play (and of any particular well, for that matter) so important to an energy company's behavior.

Further, when you consider the ratio of price of natural gas to oil, which has been consistently favoring oil as a profit engine for energy companies, you can understand why the profitability of gas has been its own barrier to widespread promotion as an alternative (and a better alternative) to crude oil and its refined products. Oil companies have continued to view most every well with this obvious monetary bias, if they can, with their primary goal to capture and sell crude oil and a very secondary goal the similar production and marketing of associated natural gas.

Now we can understand the nature of independent "shale drillers" as being truly of two distinct kinds—and why it matters where each company has assembled its assets. If your leases are in the natural-gas-rich areas of the Marcellus, which runs through Pennsylvania and New York (such as Range Resources or EQT Corp), and your typical well produces more than 80% natural gas, you don't have much choice in your approach to the energy markets. As Figure 10.3 illustrates, your focus must be on your natural gas production, as the majority of your revenues must rely on it.

Figure 10.3.
Marcellus Play: Overwhelming Natural Gas Ratios to Oil

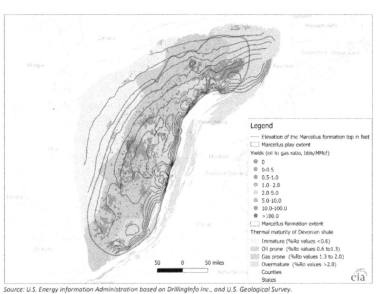

Source: U.S. Energy Information Administration based on DrillingInfo Inc., and U.S. Geological Survey.

However, if you are in the oil-rich fracking areas of West Texas or North Dakota (such as EOG Resources and Continental Resources), and your production ratio is 50%, 60%, 70%, or more oil or other liquids, you've got a choice in your strategy towards both the natural gas and oil markets. And, if your oil is worth significantly more than the natural gas you're producing—e.g., 5-10 times more—you may take the financial view that your natural gas production is little more than a waste product, not worthy of the money, time, and effort to capture and bring to market.

And that's how it has been for many U.S. shale oil companies in the Bakken and most currently in the most recent and hottest shale oil play, the Permian basin. As shale plays have continued to grow in the number of drilling rigs searching for expensive oil to bring to market, we've also seen an increasingly concurrent increase in the production of associated natural gas from those wells, as you can see from Figure 10.4.

Figure 10.4.
Associated Natural Gas Production Grows in the Oil-Rich Permian Basin

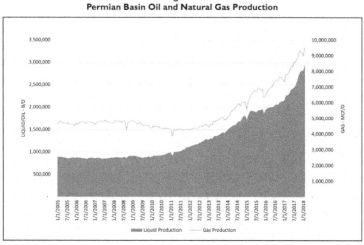

Source: PetroNerds, DrillingInfo

To energy companies looking to maximize profits from wells, this associated natural gas is a "problem" for them: the infrastructure to transport is limited and reserved for oil, prices are depressed, and capture and storage is an added expense that isn't worth the price of bringing associated natural gas to market.

This leads us to one of the most horrendous environmental and national resource offenses that's been systematically perpetrated by the oil and gas industry as any we've ever seen in the history of the United States: venting and flaring. For much of the past 15 years, oil has been worth so much more than natural gas that gas has not only been far less profitable than oil; it's actually often been an economic loser.

Imagine a gold miner who must travel through miles of zinc ore to get at his gold. Sure, the zinc is worth something on the open market, but the costs of mining that ore and transporting it just aren't worth the return, as opposed to just plowing through that ore to get at the "good stuff"—the gold.

However, with natural gas, you can't just "plow through it." It's part of every well you drill, is released when you release the oil there, and, whether you like it or not, it needs to be dealt with. If you just ignore it, like a gold miner might with the zinc he's digging up, it'll simply escape and pollute the atmosphere, which is wasteful and against environmental laws here in the United States.

So what do you do if you're a fracker in the Bakken or West Texas? You're sitting on prime oil-rich shale acreage, looking to create as much production growth and cash flow, as quickly as you can. You're trying to keep bond holders paid, keep your shareholders happy, and also keep your production goals (and your yearly bonus) intact. Meanwhile, this pesky natural gas that's coming up from your oil-rich wells is forcing you to take time and money away from all of these goals.

Your options are limited. You could suck it up, admit to a slowdown of production (and profits) and allocate pipeline volume to the associated natural gas you're producing in these wells, sending it to a major market center like the Henry Hub and getting your measly $2/mMBtu (or less) that the market is paying. The problem with this choice is that pipeline space is in very high demand in strong oil-rich fracking areas for oil volumes. Therefore, transporting natural gas can become so expensive that it can reach the market often without paying for itself with the price it commands. You can see from Figure 10.2 that nat gas, even at the Henry Hub, has rarely exceeded $2.50/mMcf in the last decade.

Not surprisingly, this is the least-appetizing option for most of these independents.

Another choice is to pay for limited transport, and try to sell the associated natural gas as close to the wellhead as possible—an option that is often the only choice for oil companies. Because of the difficulties in making a reasonable profit by transporting to a major gas nexus, many fracking companies are also trying to sell their gas locally, which causes an often-cascading collapse in those local prices as well, far worse than at bigger nexus points.

If you thought that negative prices for oil in April 2020 was a completely unheard of, unique event in the history of energy trading, I give you the last two years of local pricing for West Texas/South-East New Mexico (Waha hub) natural gas: see Figure 10.5. Here, in the most hyped, growing, and overproducing shale oil region of the United States, we've seen prices of associated natural gas from those wells move in negative territory three times in the last two years, and more often hover near zero than nearer to an already dirt-cheap Henry Hub price of $2-4/mMBtu.

Figure 10.5.
Waha Hub Natural Gas Prices (May 2018-June 2020)

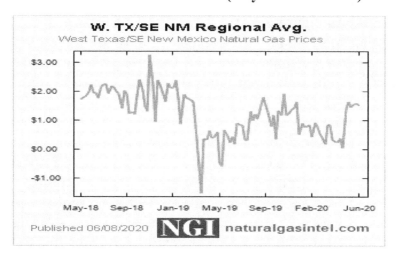

Finally, if transport to a local nexus or a more national one is cost-prohibitive, an energy company can try to get approval for the most wasteful, but likely most efficacious solution: venting or flaring.

Figure 10.6.
Escalating U.S. Natural Gas Venting and Flaring (2000-2020)

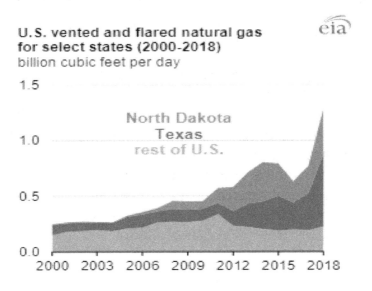

As shown in Figure 10.6, this has been the fastest-growing option that most oil and gas companies have attempted to use. Venting is as obvious a procedure as it sounds: you make no effort to capture escaping natural gas, and you allow it to flow freely into the air. Some venting is inevitable in the drilling of wells, but far too often, the unavoidable venting of associated natural gas is less tightly controlled by oil and gas companies as they might try to be. As tightly as any venting of associated gas might be regulated by state commissions, it requires very intense observation and measurements to assure that energy companies are adhering to guidelines, which few state agencies have either the resources or desire to do. This "oops" factor in associated gas venting surely makes the calculated volumes of vented associated gas in oil-rich shale areas far lower than they are in reality.

Where venting truly makes its most egregious effect is in the practice of drilled but uncompleted wells (DUCs, which I described earlier, in Chapter 9). DUC portfolios grow when oil prices tend to weaken, but when ongoing oil projects cannot be immediately stopped. Often the well is completed and prepared for production, but it's capped and left ready to resume active output when prices improve. The problem is that DUCs are particularly apt to vent associated natural gas, as it is particularly difficult to restrain the leaking of gas once it has been already stimulated from between its shale layers below.

Figures for this level of vented associated gas from DUCs range all over the place, with environmental groups claiming massive percentages of up to 15% of all gas production in the Permian, while state regulatory agencies claim well under 1%. We can guess a number that's somewhere in the middle (but likely closer to the environmentalists claims), but in all cases, it is a huge and useless waste of a valuable natural resource that can be prevented and needs to end.

The other "waste" strategy for associated gas is flaring. Flaring is simply burning, at the wellhead, the associated natural gas as it is released. You've often seen pictures of this as applied to refineries, where small parts of the refinery products that are neither valuable nor renewable are lit at the chimney top. I have images in my youth of riding past the refineries off of the New Jersey Turnpike in Carteret and Rahway on my way back from my aunt's house, watching the light show of a dozen or so tall exhaust stacks flaring hydrocarbon remains. But there's nothing romantic, or necessary, about the widespread use of natural gas flaring for the mere purpose of maximizing drilling speed and profits in West Texas and elsewhere.

Figure 10.7 is a chart from the Texas Railroad Commission (RRC), the statewide agency that (despite its name) has little to do with railroads, instead imposing the state's oil and gas industry guidelines for production. Its mandate is to "serve Texas through the stewardship of natural resources and the environment." However, during the last several years of parabolic fracking activity in Texas, the RRC has for the most part abandoned its own "Statewide Rule 32," which bans all flaring with rare exception. Figure 10.7 was part of an analysis report of RRC Commissioner Ryan Sitton in response to environmental group calls to enforce that ban. And, even using the industry advocacy RRC's analysis, it can be seen how rapidly flaring has increased with oil production.

Figure 10.7.
Rising Flaring with Production Volumes in Texas (1980-2017)

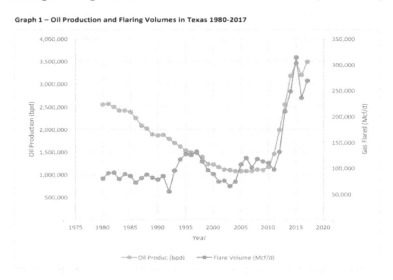

However, Figure 10.7 doesn't begin to tell the story: while total flaring statistics from the RRC put Texas flaring and venting at more than 650,000 Mmcf/day, satellite data indicates that this number is under counted by at least a factor of two in

Texas alone. To put that in perspective, the difference between those amounts is enough to power two major cities in the U.S. each and every year. Despite its mandate to limit flaring permits, the RRC has approved 27,000(!) permits to oil and gas companies to flare and vent gas since 2013, even while admitting that these permits create an "incentive to flare out of convenience and economics rather than necessity."

I would note that Texas is hardly the only state with a history of allowing flagrant waste of natural gas through venting and flaring. In the Bakken, flaring of natural gas reached a pinnacle of 30% of natural gas production, which was only slowed by South Dakota state-wide regulation enforcement after many years of mismanagement.

It is important (and not surprising) to note that the largest offenders of Rule 32 in Texas (and the most likely to apply for and be granted flaring permits) are the smaller and less-well-capitalized oil and gas companies in operation. These are the companies that are likely the most overleveraged and in need of ever-increasing cash flow, as described in Chapter 6 on shale economics. If you measure the amount of flared gas for every barrel of oil produced for all the fracking companies working in West Texas, that ratio is highest in many smaller names you've probably never heard of, such as Primexx, MDC, Exco, and Trinity. On the other side of the ledger are larger independents who, for the most part, respect Rule 32 and try to keep gas venting and flaring to a minimum, including many names you are far more likely to recognize: Pioneer, EOG, Occidental, and Devon.

I'll come back to the point of why it's so important to recognize the difference in behavior between small- and large-scale frackers as we reach for possible solutions in Chapter 11, but the most important point is just how unfathomably stupid it is to permit the kind of waste and environmental damage that venting or flaring of natural gas of any amount allows. It's like the horrible feeling we get when we see videos of mismanaged grain shipments rotting on a dock, or the vast amounts of food that get thrown out from restaurants at the end of the day, while millions of Americans go to bed hungry.

The environmental damage of natural gas venting and flaring is obvious. But the waste of natural gas is equally bad in two other ways. First, natural gas is a limited resource: you cannot replant gas under the ground as you can renew a harvest for wheat. Second (and this may be even more disturbing), these are resources that the United States is going to be desperate to have at a point not so far into the future. No matter what the biases and barriers to natural gas use that remain today, there is no doubt that we all will rely in the near future on a larger and more significant percentage of natural gas to power our lives. The waste of venting and flaring natural gas is a national resources disaster that's happening today—one that can be reduced, if not completely stopped, on a national level with a little smart planning.

The case for moving our country towards more dependence on natural gas and less on oil is incredibly one-sided: it is cheaper, it's cleaner, it's more abundant, and it can replicate virtually any use that crude oil and its refined products can, while requiring minimal processing from wellhead to burner. In a country like ours with our vast pipeline networks, the price remains relatively constant throughout the network, and those prices are not subject to foreign geopolitical disturbances.

Finally, and this may be most important: all renewable sources are electricity sources, and they must rely on a secondary electricity source to supplement them. Wind doesn't always blow, and the sun doesn't shine at night. In the advocacy for alternative energy that is sustainable, you cannot have a conversion of measure without considering these secondary/supplementary sources as well.

And natural gas is, far and away, the most "natural" one for that task. Yes, if you are really serious about increasing our reliance on renewable energy and not just mouthing "green rhetoric," you'd better take very seriously at least one fossil fuel: natural gas.

CHAPTER 11:

TURNING OIL GREEN

R enewable energy is on the rise all over the globe. Everybody is far more aware and energized about our climate change challenge. Every newspaper and media outlet sports its own "Green" section, and even oil companies are touting zero-emission plans. There's little doubt where our future lies, not even to the most confirmed climate change denier and fossil fuel advocate: we'll be a country of sustainable energy at some point. We have to be.

I often feel somewhat left out of this revolution, a lifetime observer and analyst of 'quaint' oil and gas in the midst of an obviously barreling "green" freight train coming down the tracks, its lights growing brighter and brighter in the distance, about to mow down the remnants of "dirty" oil and its evil advocates. No one even bothers to mention fossil fuels in their plans for renewables anymore, thinking – naively – that the road to solar, wind, and geothermal power is completely independent of the already well-traveled highway of fossil fuels and their refined products. We take oil and gas, the energy they provide and their integrated processes for chemicals, pharmaceuticals, plastics, asphalt, glass – ad infinitum – so much for granted now that we can almost ignore them. And we do.

But this won't work. There is a reality here we cannot ignore – not if we really want to see that sustainable future appear as fast as we can. We can't ignore these fossil fuels as we push towards a solution to our climate crisis.

Figure 11.1.
Global Share of Wind and Solar Electricity Generation (2015-2020)

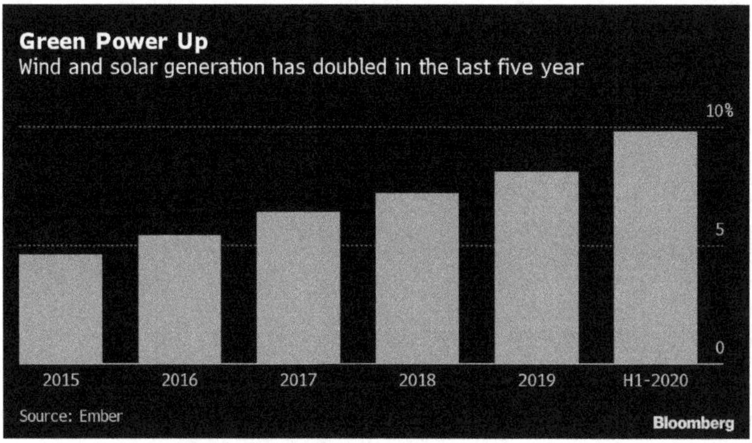

While we've made tremendous progress in renewable fuel sources as shown in figure 11.1, doubling its global market share percentage in the last five years, even the most optimistic predictions on these renewable sources show it falling far short of the vast development it needs to meet climate goals and continue to double every five years. And I fear that the vast endemic oil surplus caused by the coronavirus pandemic will set that timeline even further back than these projections currently estimate.

Figure 11.2 is about as good a representation as I can find of the still very long road that renewables need to travel to become a really significant part of our energy mix.

Figure 11.2.
The Long Road for Renewables

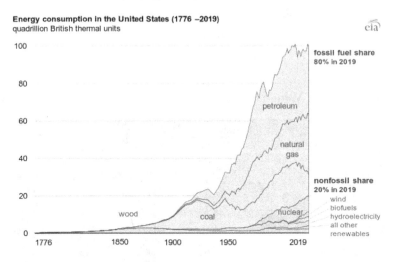

Energy consumption in the United States (1776 –2019)
quadrillion British thermal units

Although 2019 was a record for "non-fossil fuel" share of energy use, once you remove the near 10% of nuclear power, the contribution from real renewable sources is still pathetic, even with the quick and continuing decline of coal. If we're going to really combat climate change, we're going to have to move a lot faster.

Environmental groups have drawn a clear line on global warming as a measurement of advancing climate change—and that is to avoid an increase in global temperatures of 1.5 degrees Celsius, as laid out in the Paris Accords. Temperatures have been measured to have increased already by 1 degree Celsius since the turn of the century, leaving only another 0.5 degree of room before this benchmark is reached. This trending hashtag of #105C accompanies many of the daily tweets and other social media posts I see, a rational benchmark that environmentalists agree represents a tipping point of disaster from which there is no return. Tropical heat waves, the source of extreme events like hurricane season in the Fall are doubled, extending those seasons by a month and the melting of

Greenland's polar sheet becomes irreversible – these are only two of the many scary projections accompanying the 1.5C benchmark.

A half of a degree, It leaves little room (or time) for error. Some major changes need to be made, and made now.

In the previous pages, I've tried to lay the groundwork for a different kind of approach to the problem—and a more practical one—than virtually every other program or suggestion I've seen to date. In every case, there's been an attack on the symptoms of increasing global fossil fuel use and its contributions to carbon and global warming, like the attack on oil companies and oil production, and very little looking to attack and ultimately solve the underlying disease, which is the relentless economic appetite for those fossil fuels.

Here's an example of what I think is the wrong way that this fight is being waged: In June 2020, the IEA released a special examination of its yearly World Energy Outlook (WEO), reporting on the global use of fossil fuels and the likely scenarios for demand for oil and gas following the COVID-19 pandemic. Its purpose was to lay out possible scenarios to move global energy use towards renewables, seeing the pandemic as a possible opportunity to "reboot" the trajectory of oil and gas demand. It makes several possible suggestions to governments on initiatives it might undertake to push the renewable agenda forward, including several boilerplate suggestions we've all seen before, including modernizing electricity grids, creating incentives for EVs, reducing methane emission, and phasing out fossil-fuel-drilling incentives. Good ideas, all.

But with this, as with virtually every other projection that the IEA WEO has done (and every other predictive model I have seen anywhere, regardless of the source), the report reiterates its previous projection for demand growth for oil to resume at near the benchmark increase of 1 million barrels a day per year, once the virus and its associated slowdown has run its course. This is a number I have referred to often in this book, not because I want it to be true, but because, without several changes to the global marketplace for oil and gas, and without a financial reason to do so, I believe it has little hope of dropping significantly merely by ranting in horror at it.

On the other hand, maybe the COVID-19 pandemic will represent a 'new normal,' where energy demand never fully recovers to where it was previously. Maybe the world will embrace 'work at home' and cut commuting, or forever eat out at restaurants less or fly less often on airlines, or cut music and other show traffic by 15% or more, even after a reliable vaccine is found. I don't know.

But even this possible outcome only throws more cold water on the progress of renewables. We've seen that because of the pandemic, oil demand has dropped suddenly worldwide, expanding the surpluses of oil exponentially. This was the major reason that prices for oil briefly went negative in April 2020, but that's not even the major point. The real issue is that further surpluses in oil will naturally keep oil prices down, likely for a long time to come until those surpluses clear – if they ever now fully clear. And I hope I've convinced you of at least one thing in this book: As long as cheap oil is easily had, there's little financial incentive to move smartly towards renewable development and deployment.

Meanwhile, as the WEO report was released, my Twitter screen lit up with expected complaints from every well-meaning environmental group in reaction to this "sustainability" report from the IEA. The Sierra Club, 350.org, Oil Change International, and the Energy Watch Group all peppered the Internet with hashtags to #fixtheWEO, complaining that their demand projections—and their sustainability suggestions—all would become a self-fulfilling prophesy, are far too superficial to matter, are designed to support the oil and gas industry, and need to "be realigned" to the Paris goals of avoiding that 1.5C temperature rise.

This targeting of the IEA's annual report by environmentalists has been going on for nearly a decade, consuming time and energy uselessly. If there ever were a case of *shooting the messenger*, this seemed to me to be one of the most obvious examples. Sure, the IEA is often correctly seen as an advocacy arm for the fossil fuel industry. But its power to change decision-making inside of the oil and gas industry (and inside governments) is grossly overestimated. For the most part, the IEA is a toothless recorder of the world's energy demand and supplies in all its forms, and a pretty fair reporter of what it finds at that.

To me, the IEA's projections provide the raw data that environmentalists should use to convince industry and governments that their actions on climate change are misdirected and far, far too slow. They should then thank the IEA for its honest assessments and turn elsewhere for solutions that will arrest the increasing demand for fossil fuels and further increase the market share for wind and solar power. Attacking the projections seems to me as close to attacking science as groups who purportedly promote science themselves might ever like to come.

Further, IEA suggestions to tackle climate change are completely inconsequential. Its boilerplate suggestions, which could have been written by anyone with a cursory understanding of energy, prove the IEA's talents lie for the most part in collating and projecting numbers.

No, if you want to really want to change the trajectory of oil demand and you need to do it now, there's one surefire way to do it: Make oil prices so high that renewable sources are more than competitive, they're financially superior to fossil fuels. Then, keep oil prices high, by removing the often-repeating market conditions that precede the disasters that continue to plague oil prices, running them back and forth on an ever-recurring treadmill of boom and bust.

Most of the financial assets in the world have normally tracked inflation—that is, all except for oil and natural gas, which have been uniquely absent from this pattern. Real estate goes ever higher, as do stocks and gold, coffee, and wood. But oil and gas remain outside of that norm for a few crazy reasons I've tried to examine, cycling endlessly between unnaturally high and ridiculously low prices since the futures markets were deregulated and the advent of shale drilling began in the early 2000s. It's time for all of that to change, for the benefit of consumers, oil companies, shareholders, and of course, our planet.

We've got a U.S. independent oil industry that's infused with the "American Capitalist Spirit." By that, I mean that many of the independent oil companies are run by lone entrepreneurial leaders who have struck out on their own, usually with little beginning capital, and have created fantastic successes in the oil patch. These companies, and the people leading them, are seen as the best examples of America's competitive edge, heroes, the kind of Horatio Alger story that inspires us all. Leaders in state and federal government have given deference to these stories and these companies, delivering every advantage of regulatory freedoms, as have the analysts and investors in the major banks, credit houses, and outside Wall Street, who have hyped their stories and given access to nearly unlimited capital for nearly two decades.

The U.S. shale boom has similarly captured the imagination of the country and our government, with its hopes of new American jobs and commerce and the further dream of U.S. energy independence from foreign sources. The hope of this independence joins, for one brief moment, the Right and the Left, and while the Right generally seeks more oil and gas from here in the U.S. and the Left seeks more domestic renewable supplies, both want to end the need for energy coming from the powder keg Middle East, where geopolitical difficulties continue to ensnare the United States to waste both economic and military resources.

Both of these myths of American derring-do in the energy patch and the quest for energy "independence" need to be recognized for the nonsense they are and exploded. Our national and state governments have bent over far too much to accommodate oil companies, particularly in the hot shale zones of the Bakken and the Permian, allowing all manner of environmentally unfriendly activities that have accelerated their production astronomically—and destructively—in shale. Compliance in regulations on spacing, methane leaking, DUCs, venting and flaring, wastewater and tailponding, river dumping, fracking fluid chemistry, cementing, and so many others continue to be of issue in the oil patch. But, even after deference to many of these issues by regulators, very little to increase the profitability of shale producers has emerged, while helping a simultaneous crash in prices twice in the last five years, which instead of helping frackers, helped bankrupt them. Oil companies are clearly their own worst enemies, and their greed and bad management have combined to not only negatively impact their shareholders, but slow the natural progression towards renewable fuels.

The approach from Washington toward shale, and U.S. energy policy in general, has been no better. Since the days of the fuel crisis of the '70s and Richard Nixon, no American president has done much to establish a national policy approach that purposely moves our energy progression along, from oil and natural gas to solar and wind and other renewables, just as it has from wood and horsepower to coal and water generation to oil before it. Mostly, there's been a load of talk of the wonders of the U.S. energy industry from both Democrat and Republican presidents, a nod towards the "need" for energy independence, and a natural instinct of malleability with pretty much everything that oil

companies have lobbied for. Even the most obvious (and necessary) attempts at arresting oil and gas excesses, such as President Obama's EPA initiatives on coal plants and other emissions,
CAFE regulations, and dozens of others were quickly reversed by
the Trump administration.

The time for the piecemeal approach to energy promotion and
regulation by the Federal government that changes every time
the occupant of the White House changes needs to end. With a
firm plan and timeline, both the oil industry as well as environmentalists can correctly figure and cope with the transitions and
the speed at which that conversion can reasonably happen. Oil
companies—particularly major oil companies like Exxon, Chevron, Shell, and BP—can budget their targets exactly for transi-
tioning away from oil towards gas and renewables and be a part
of the global solution, instead of an adversary and roadblock to
it. And they have shown that they're ready to be. Figure 11.3
shows the commitment of European majors to investment in renewable energy, with French giant Total and Dutch major Shell
expending 15% of their total budgets towards renewables as
soon as 2021. U.S. majors aren't far behind.

Figure 11.3.
European Majors' Percentage of Renewables Spending

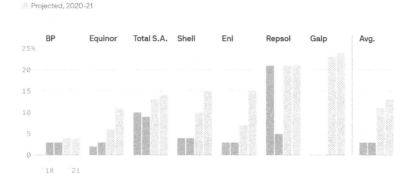

European oil companies' clean energy
investments as a share of capital spending

Even with this unprecedented recent push of capital towards renewable energy by the majors, it's clearly not been enough, not
nearly. We need to incentivize this investment further—much
further—with other market and policy changes far different from
the ones we've relied on in the past.

All of the standard initiatives that have been discussed so often
among environmentalists and been vaguely outlined in the
Democratic "Green New Deal" are worthy goals to work for, but
none of them chart a method for achieving any of those initiatives. I've done a lot of moaning to both sides of the political
spectrum, almost equally excoriating greedy and incompetent
shale oil players as I have the environmental lobby. But nothing
has been as unachievable and frankly useless as the "Green New
Deal" resolution.

I know that the Green New Deal resolution was intended to be
an opening salvo for discussions on the political directions that
the U.S. Congress can take to help push our country towards renewables and mitigating climate change. But even with this lack
of commitment that H.R. 109 demands, these proposals strike
me as pure Alice-in-Wonderland fantasy: 100% renewable energy, without a fossil fuel of any kind in sight, net-zero emissions,
eliminating pollution completely, mitigating storm risk (caused
by global warming), cleaning of waste sites. All of these are part
of the far-reaching 'plan,' and there is more that goes well beyond energy policy, including calls for a universal living wage,
free health care, and affordable housing. It even includes a
shout-out for American Indian protesters of the Keystone pipeline project, requiring "the free and informed consent" of indig-
enous peoples who are affected by pipelines and other
infrastructure projects needing government agency approval. As
for any mention of the multi-trillion-dollar budgetary additions
that would be necessary to even begin to achieve these goals, the
Green New Deal is completely lacking.

Even for a liberal observer who would very much like to see many of these goals accomplished, the resolution does appear as little more than a political stunt, designed to measure support in the Congress and in the public of every left-wing wish-list item possible, but with zero hope of success.

We've got to do better than this and begin prescribing solutions that actually are achievable; that benefit both the environment as well as the mid-manager working at the pipeline company; that will push the nation forwards towards renewable energy as well as benefit the pensioners who depend on the dividends from their ownership of Conoco-Philips and Shell oil shares.

As I've said over and over again, the quickest way to do this is push fossil fuel prices higher, and most notably in crude oil, which will incentivize not only the continued conversion to natural gas, but also vastly accelerate the interest and money spent to develop the more far-reaching infrastructure needed to make solar and wind power a more significant part of our energy mix. In every area of the energy chain, there are achievable goals that benefit both the oil company and the environmentalist, both the right and the left, and can be done in a bi-partisan way.

Let me be clear: I am a liberal, and my recommendations begin with the thought that while capitalism is what has made this country's economy the strongest in the world, unfettered and unregulated capitalism has a long history of creating fundamental inequalities and excesses that have hurt workers and our environment in equal measure. In the oil patch, I hope I've proven that these excesses are now helping to destroy the very planet we all occupy, and some needed controls are demanded to put things right again. I also strongly believe that controls of these sorts, when well-thought-out and applied, are precisely what governments are obligated to do, for the sake of its country's citizens and their children of future generations. With that, let's start with the oil companies.

FIXING U.S. SHALE OIL

I've hopefully made it clear that what I believe has primarily stopped oil from reaching and maintaining triple-digit prices over the last 15 years are the excesses of the (relatively infant) U.S. shale sector. The model that's emerged for shale oil and gas production requires little initial investment and flourishes when capital is cheap. Sign a lease, go to the bank and get a loan on the projected earnings for drilling, and off you go. This has led to sector-wide abuse of debt and leverage, a "Ponzi scheme" of ever-increasing production, and bulging surpluses of overproduction that have crashed the global oil price three times since 2014. In order to stop this wasteful cycling for good, we've got to get these assets into the hands of better-capitalized and disciplined managers—managers who don't need to drill at full speed at all times to cover bond and other debt payments, nor show investors growth at any cost at the expense of returns.

To fix this, we've got to incentivize the transfer/sale/consolidation of independent shale oil companies towards the better-capitalized majors, and disincentivize the start-up and ramping up of small, independent shale drillers using massive debt. This consolidating has been happening naturally since 2014, courtesy of those three bust cycles, but with continuing access to more and more cheap capital, it's been happening far too slowly. The timeline on climate change is short, and we need to accelerate this process wherever we can.

The simplest way to do that is to put guardrails on domestic oil production, as we have put guardrails on banks who equally have engaged in leveraged speculation, with disastrous results. Capital requirements for oil independents to drill wells are long past due, where there should be an established debt-to-equity minimum to operations. This will force smaller E&Ps to restrain capex and production when oil prices are lower, while allowing slower and more conservative expansion when they are higher.

The outlines for these capital restrictions might perhaps find a middle road between the debt to equity ratios of current independents and the same ratios for current US majors. Infant independent oil companies should not have to meet the economic elasticity of companies that have been in business for more than a century, but also should not be allowed to continue to operate solely on credit and a prayer of higher oil prices. For those producers who have lived on the edge of credit while waiting for oil prices to recover, the likelihood of needing an equity partner with better capital resources under these limitations greatly increases, or even the chances of bankruptcy in a price downturn. But this is precisely what we want. Minimum capital requirements will necessarily slow the breakneck expansion that has become the theme of independent oil production, and it will force producers to bring oil to market only when it produces a reasonable profit. It will also force those less well-capitalized players into the arms of those that are better equipped financially, whether those folks are the big majors like Exxon and Chevron, or corporations normally outside of the energy space but with a history of investment in seemingly unrelated sectors, such as multi-faceted conglomerates like GE and United Technologies.

The rationales for capital restraints on oil companies don't quite quote the exact same song lyrics as it was with the banks that was undertaken with Dodd-Frank reforms after the financial crisis of 2008, but they certainly rhyme. While ongoing risks to the general economy of overleveraged banks were the main factor in applying minimum capital requirements on those deemed "too big to fail," we can say that the risks to both the waste of our sovereign, irreplaceable natural resources and the safety of the environment are equally worthy reasons to apply these guidelines, if not more so.

With shale assets in stronger hands, the need for constantly increasing volume-busting production targets mostly disappears. Well-capitalized majors are not forced to consistently increase production based on the risk of credit pressures and have long-term, more disciplined, and conservative E&P plans in development and growth that smaller independents simply cannot duplicate. Chevron wants to be here for the long haul, while many small independent producers have frankly been "bought to be sold." Majors are better equipped to 'ride out' downturns in prices, cutting away profitless production, whereas smaller players are actually financially forced to push forwards and increase even marginally profitable oil drilling, especially during bad times. By being better financed and able to chart a longer-term course, majors cutting production in a downturn make those downturns less severe and shorter lived. Oil prices stay higher, come down less when they do come down, and resume an upwards path again more quickly.

We also need national oversight on fracking that supersedes state agencies, and particularly in the area of natural gas venting and flaring. Except in operational cases where it cannot be avoided, there should be national regulations that forbid, except for inevitable operational losses, the venting and flaring of associated natural gas. There is no excuse for the waste of our sovereign natural resources that venting and flaring have caused in the boom age of shale oil production. We're going to need that gas, and soon. We simply cannot allow it to be thrown away, causing excess pollution without delivering its energy benefits into our economy.

It is merely because of greed and the bankrupted model of oil fracking that venting and flaring of natural gas is estimated to be 15% of the current recovered supply here in the U.S. If you don't have the infrastructure available to safely transport associated natural gas to a market nexus, then you simply should not be allowed to take the associated oil out of that hole.

And if you're unwilling to move associated natural gas to market because it's a financial loser, then again, too bad: you should not be able to sell the oil that's sitting there with the gas, either – no matter how high that oil is being priced.

The positives to prohibiting venting and flaring would be huge and immediate. Producers would be forced to market all associated natural gas, making many fracked oil wells unprofitable and shutting them down during price plunges. This would not only increase the prices for natural gas, which we have seen often run near zero and even negatively precisely where U.S. oil fracking is hottest (for example, in the Waha hub), it would also cut production and help increase prices of crude oil similarly. All of this while gaining a major anti-pollution benefit of stopping the criminal waste of natural gas by merely releasing it into the atmosphere or burning it at the wellhead.

To tie these two proposals together, the consolidation of shale assets into stronger hands helps with the slowing of flared associated natural gas as well. We have seen that the biggest offenders of flaring are precisely the smallest independents, which are hell-bent on securing the quickest profits on higher priced shale oil and are most willing to apply for flaring permits from state agencies like the Texas RRC, tossing away associated gas.

As long as we're talking about the deliberate waste of natural gas, let's talk a little about unintended waste: the leaking of natural gas from local and interstate pipelines. This has been a tougher issue to approach because leaks are a part of pipeline operations. Unfortunately, everything leaks, at least a little. Further, natural gas leaks are more difficult than oil leaks to discover and fix. When oil leaks, it's obviously apparent and impossible to ignore. But when natural gas leaks, it's invisible.

The EPA estimates that 1.4% of all natural gas that comes out of the ground disappears into the atmosphere before reaching its endpoint. A 2018 study by Colorado State University estimates that number is 60% greater—that is, 2.3%—which represents a loss of 13 million cubic tons of methane a year.

The technology of rapid detection exists to do far better than this, even if we cannot possibly eliminate leaking natural gas completely. And we must do better. An Environmental Defense Fund study estimates that once methane leakage exceeds 3%, the atmospheric damage it causes mitigates the advantages natural-gas-fired power plants have over coal.

I'm not sure if those comparative numbers are reliable, but surely we must maximize the environmental advantages of moving towards natural gas as much as we can. Again, the benefits besides to the environment are clear: increasing costs of getting natural gas to market increases the break-even prices of natural gas wells and oil wells with significant associated gas, helping to shut off production and sending prices of both higher.

For the shale oil and gas industry, my suggestions include capital restraints, a ban on flaring and venting, and better regulation of leaking methane. For the oil and gas folks ready to have my head on a platter for all these recommendations, I have other recommendations they'll surely like better, involving natural gas.

YES, VIRGINIA, THERE IS A SANTA CLAUS – TRANSITIONAL NATURAL GAS

I met Boone Pickens twice in my life. He was the prototypical wildcatter. He understood the nuts and bolts of the industry, from the differences in the dirt that held all of that oil and gas, to the Wall Street firms who ran the numbers game at the futures markets that put prices on all that energy. He was a fund manager, and he got a lot of grief for pushing forwards his fa-mous "Pickens plan," which advocated natural gas, while he held massive stakes in natural gas companies.

But he was right: natural gas was the correct way for the U.S. to move our energy portfolio forwards, both when he introduced the plan in 2008 and even more so today. Natural gas is cleaner, more abundant, and far cheaper than oil. It solves the "problem" of U.S. energy independence by placing domestic energy sup-plies higher up the ladder as a more dominant fossil fuel supply, displacing Middle East oil. Even in the most aggressive develop-ment scenario for renewables, there remains a huge reliance on fossil fuels at least until 2050. And even then, the technology of batteries and capacitors will have to have come a long way to dis-place fossil fuels as auxiliary supplies to wind and solar. The sun doesn't shine at night, and the wind blows when it wants to. Sup-plemental energy from fossil fuels will be a part of our energy portfolio, likely forever. If that's the case, doesn't it make sense to move the grid as close to a carbon-neutral fossil fuel as you can find? That's indisputably natural gas.

The ignorance of the public towards natural gas has to change, particularly the rhetoric and propaganda of the "green" lobby of the left-wing of the Democratic party. Natural gas is not just an-other fossil fuel, to be placed in the same general hopper with, for example, filthy tar-sands oil. The environmental push to ban fracking in all its forms, without regard to where that fracking is taking place and those specific geographical environmental risks and whether that fracking is primarily for oil or natural gas has been destructive to the evolutionary flow of our energy mix away from far dirtier and more dangerous liquids toward natural gas. Proponents of the Green New Deal (and the latest-announced Democratic green initiatives) should instead correctly view nat-ural gas as a stepping-stone towards renewables, and not as the enemy of sustainable energy.

For the energy industry, a serious move towards natural gas from oil helps to upgrade the thousands of secondary assets that contain a more significant gas-to-oil ratio (a far larger group than those currently being drilled) that have languished in company portfolios in recent years. It shifts the focus of energy E&Ps from a one-sided obsession on liquids to a far more equal and therefore far more natural and cost-effective mix of both oil and natural gas. This will reduce the recent tendency to prefer oily assets and treat its gassy second sister as a mere waste product to be pushed aside. In production, it makes natural gas a valued part of the well's output to be marketed alongside its more expensive brother, and it therefore encourages better efforts in controlling leakage, venting, and flaring, even without regulations.

As opposed to the advanced renewable technology on solar panels, batteries, and capacitors that doesn't yet exist today, the technology for greatly reducing the current problems with natural gas certainly does. Better cementing, valving, piping, waste disposal, and detection efforts can mitigate many of the issues with natural gas fracking, and a consolidated effort of promotion of natural gas, along with tighter regulatory efforts in these areas, is a package deal that both environmentalists and the oil and gas industry should be very quick to agree to. From the federal government, there should be incentives towards the production of natural gas over oil, rebates for natural-gas-powered trucks and buses, and easier approval for infrastructure spending for natural gas pipelines, pulling some of the decisions away from the slow-motion court system. On the other side, the EPA should apply and enforce stricter regulations regarding natural gas well fracked wastewater treatment and removal, venting and flaring, and methane leakage, both with DUCs and during pipeline transport.

The moment for natural-gas-powered automobiles seems to have passed, a possibility perhaps when Boone first proposed his "Pickens plan" but not now in the modern age of EVs. But the efficacy of natural-gas-powered trucks is still wildly more advantageous than electric trucks, where batteries for long-hauling are still too bulky and heavy to make realistic truck loads at realistic long-haul distances possible. The federal government could boost trucks (which are still more than 1/8 of total U.S. emissions) towards conversion from diesel to natural gas with tax credits, as well as help defray the costs of interstate truck-stop additions of natural-gas-refueling pumps. Adding a natural gas line into any service station is a relatively cheap upgrade that would pay for itself almost immediately in cleaner emissions and cheaper fuel costs.

If this country's politicians are truly serious about energy independence, they could attain it far more easily by promoting natural gas than by promoting drilling on federally owned lands and fighting wars in the Middle East. The more our economy shifts towards domestic natural gas, the less it will rely on non-domestic oil supplies.

In the energy world, and in the world in general (and for the past 20 years, at least), the move towards natural gas has been a literal no-brainer. The climate crisis makes this only more compulsory. There are no excuses anymore.

THE U.S. GOVERNMENT NEEDS A CONSISTENT POLICY TOWARDS ENERGY

Our government needs a consolidated energy policy and has for decades: one that doesn't change depending on who is in the White House. That probably means legislation, instead of the executive orders and initiatives that come from the executive branch and are carried out through federal agencies such as the EPA, transport, commerce, treasury, and energy departments. A bi-partisan commission with legislative suggestions might be a useful start, even if these commissions have most often been plagued by failure. Even the vaunted Bowles-Simpson plan of fiscal reform of 2010 resulted in little; however, at least it was an honest discussion of the problems and possible real solutions to them. Let me make some suggestions as to the possible outline of such a commission.

From the Green New Deal, there could be a renewal of unshakable commitment to the Paris Climate Accords, one that cannot be breached by any executive. There could also be incentives and a budget for development of solar, wind, and EV technologies, and a target for a 100% carbon neutral electricity grid.

To incentivize fossil fuel advocates, there could be equal federal incentives for converting from oil and coal to using natural gas in electric generating power plants and truck transportation. There should be a federal statute that releases oil companies from mandated production of oil and gas leases. We need to give energy companies an option to drill based on market conditions, instead of a requirement that is handcuffing them from producing only when the market warrants it. Further, the U.S. government can and should deliver some market protections from OPEC when it tries to manipulate prices solely in order to destroy U.S. oil competition, using tariffs on Saudi and other foreign oil. We should also have a method for making approval of natural gas pipelines and other infrastructure far easier and expediting foot-dragging court cases against pipeline owners.

We need to remove the billions of dollars of oil subsidies that have long ago done their job to develop oil and gas production when it was vital to the U.S. economy. We also need to replace those subsidies with others that promote renewable energy sources. But here's the catch: We need to give those subsidies with preference back to the fossil-fuel energy companies that are losing them. In our development battle for renewables, there are no better organizations suited than the energy companies that understand the marketing, transport, and distribution of energy in all its forms.

Of the estimated $20b in energy subsidies that oil and gas companies now receive and might stand now to lose, each company should be entitled to continue to receive them equally for an equal investment in the development of wind, solar, or other sustainable energy. This will ensure current fossil fuel companies have added "skin in the game" to be an aggressive part of our shift towards renewables, and not a natural roadblock to it.

From the U.S. government, I know this is a lot to ask. It requires a bi-partisan approach that forces both fossil-fuel advocates and environmentalists to a negotiating table together, something that some might think of as impossibly unlikely. But outlines for immutable energy policy that benefit everyone, while forcing concessions from everyone, are the most likely to have lasting power and lasting benefit. It is certain that other proposals that have unilaterally benefited oil companies or environmentalists in the past have arrived "dead," with no chance of success. It's time to make a deal.

FIXING THE BANKRUPT ENERGY MARKETS

I've pointedly stayed away from the major energy proposals that have continued to make the circuits throughout the U.S. and Europe in tackling climate change over the last decade, including carbon trading, gasoline taxes, nuclear power and nuclear waste, carbon sequestration techniques, and so on. I have opinions on all of them, and I believe each could be very useful in helping us move towards a renewable future. But I've avoided talking about them for a reason. It's because I know relatively little about all of them, and several experts have written far more wisely on all these ideas than I ever could.

However, on the nature of energy markets, I've spent a lifetime as an observer and participant in them, and I think I bring a unique and useful perspective. My first book, *Oil's Endless Bid*, was a description of the financialization of oil that began in the early 2000s— and brought evidence that the prices of oil often and for long periods did not represent fundamental supply and demand. Since derivatives were deregulated by the Commodity Futures Modernization Act (CFMA, signed in 2000 by President Clinton), oil prices saw fundamentals often swept aside by financial influences instead. *Oil's Endless Bid* was a description of how futures markets—that is, commodity derivatives—created a bankrupt system for determining the prices of a vitally important commodity to all of us.

Recent negative prices of oil in April 2020 represented the other price extreme, proving again how bankrupt the global oil pricing system remains. It was not only the financial excesses leading up to the economic collapse of 2008 that drove oil prices ridiculously high towards $150 a barrel that shows this failure. It was also the unlikely and frankly ridiculous lack of an insignificant couple of million barrels of adequate storage in one small U.S. hub that sent global prices to an unbelievable negative $37 a barrel this year. The mechanisms of futures trading—which were intended to be a free-market method of price discovery—have long since proven to be far too often abused by manipulation, or financial inputs that should have nothing to do with the price of oil, or the mere stupidity of too few empty storage tanks. Moreover, prices can literally come off the rails from any of these "glitches"—sometimes for a few days and – as has been the case - sometimes for years. This pricing system has become a burden for oil companies and oil users alike looking to correctly price their costs or their profits, benefiting no one except perhaps the exchanges taking commissions and computerized hedge funds making millions on the daily billions of micro-cent trades.

Figure 11.4 charts the S+P 500 from the year 2000 on. I could have chosen car prices, or housing, or coffee or just about any other asset class as a reference. Figure 11.5 charts oil prices during the same time period.

Figure 11.4.
S&P 500 Index (2000 - 2020)

Figure 11.5. Oil Prices (2000 - 2020)

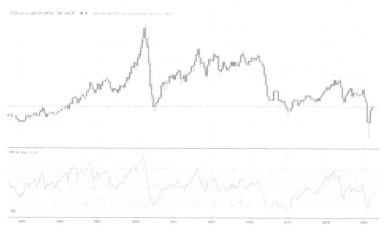

What's wrong with this picture?

Like most asset classes during the amazing growth period that has so far defined the new millennium, stocks have mostly gone up, keeping pace with growth and inflation everywhere. But oil? Since 2000, it has been on a roller-coaster ride, cycling between outrageously expensive prices that then crash to ridiculously low prices, and back up again. When did oil prices actually correctly represent the balance of supply, demand, and global growth? We all can only guess. However, clearly, $147 in 2008 was not a time that it did, nor was $27 a barrel in 2009, nor $110 in 2011, nor the recent price of negative $37 we saw in April of 2020.

The current system for oil pricing simply isn't working for anyone, and it hasn't for years. Oil companies cannot plan constructively for the development of new supplies. Users can't reasonably know what their costs will be. And the economy is ever in doubt of major effects from oil either going up berserkly or crashing fast towards zero.

But what can be done?

Despite being a participant and observer of this system for nearly 40 years, I'm hard pressed to suggest a better system. Futures markets are worthwhile price-discovery tools with a lot to recommend them, and I'm not suggesting a complete replacement of that system.

Still, I do have a few suggestions that might make oil prices a whole lot less prone to outrageous extremes. If you are reading this as a financial layperson, I'm warning you that I'm going to get a bit into the weeds here; if you hate that kind of stuff, you're welcome to skip this and move on. I won't mind.

I'm going to refer again to my previous book, *Oil's Endless Bid*. The most important and controversial case I made there was that a new class of buyers of oil as an asset class was created during the early years of the 2000s. This class comprised mostly large investment banks, and it formed a balance for the many commercial sellers of oil they had previously encountered, which were mostly oil companies. In fact, they were so successful at this that soon buyers had overrun their commercial counterparts, and as buyers swamped out the sellers, oil raged wildly higher (hence, the title of the book I ultimately settled on). As further proof of this thesis I advanced in 2011, I don't think that it's a coincidence that oil prices never again got close to the heights they did in 2008, considering the constraints on bank trading that were put into place after the financial crisis by Dodd-Frank and the slow demise and ultimate closing of most investment bank commodity trading desks. Quite simply, the "endless bid" of ever-increasing and hungrier buyers of oil has disappeared.

During the current coronavirus pandemic, we've seen an economy in utter freefall. Unemployment rages at Great Depression levels. Possible growth and profitability for many sectors of the economy look on hold for a long time to come, and some appear perhaps as if they will never recover (whether or not a fully protective vaccine is found). Until that time (which may be more than a year away), restaurants, airlines, travel, entertainment, sports, schools, and much more all seem to be on hold or at least vastly slowed. And yet, the stock market remains a mere 10% below its all-time highs. (UPDATE: New highs in the stock market were reached in August 2020.)

Why is this?

A lot of reasons can be found to attribute this strength, but surely one of the biggest is the U.S. Treasury's $1T of proposed asset purchases of U.S. companies, and even more so, its promise of virtually limitless purchases of further assets as needed to keep corporate America and the U.S. economy afloat during the crisis. Bailout? Backstop? Whatever you call this "infinite put" on the market, it's helped enormously to put a floor on stock prices and kept them high—higher than they surely ought to be. And the government has not had to resort to anywhere near this level of buying to prop up stocks: merely the promise of the U.S. Federal Reserve to support stocks has been enough to compel investors back into them. To investors, it has become quite obvious:, the government is basically limiting their possible losses, until further notice, into anything they choose to speculate on. Importantly, if you're the Fed, you also don't have to actually buy much to inspire this confidence in any class of assets; you really only have to threaten that you will. If you promise to infinitely buy assets at a lower price, you'll find no shortage of speculating investors who will 'take the chance' to bid up that asset ahead of you.

Now, take this very powerful idea of 'threatening' to backstop debt and stock assets and apply it to oil markets. Since losing the investment banks as the producer of the "endless bid" in the years after the Dodd-Frank reforms, oil markets have been searching for a replacement. And although it strikes one correctly as more than a bit of manipulation at play here, (it's no less of one in the stock and bond markets), I think there are several very good reasons to install the Federal Reserve as a "buyer of last resort" of oil to help return oil to a dependably steady and rising price.

The Strategic Petroleum Reserve (SPR) is a U.S.-controlled stored supply of oil, created in 1975 to provide a buffer for consumers and the U.S. economy in case of the type of Middle East boycott we saw in 1973. Since that time, the threat of Middle East boycotts has disappeared to nothing, both because of the development of U.S. and other North American sources, but also because of the changed geopolitics in the Middle East, which are now nothing like they were in the 1970s. Consequently, the SPR is an obsolete supply used now only for political purposes, as in to bolster an economy during election years. However, the SPR could be repurposed to serve the ends of U.S. energy policy, as a managed buyer and seller of oil, steadying its price fluctuations.

It would hardly make the U.S. Treasury (and U.S. government) as the lone sovereign nation with national commodity supplies at its control with the intent to steady domestic markets. Nations all over the world have stockpiled grain and other foodstuffs, with the opposite purpose to keep wheat, corn, and soybeans steady during price spikes, while China and India have large stockpiles of oil and copper for similar reasons. And the Strategic Petroleum Reserve here in the U.S. is already another example of a controlled supply designed to similarly buffer prices from spiking high prices. What I am suggesting is simply a secondary purposing of the SPR that will equally protect markets from the opposite extreme as well.

I am not suggesting anywhere near the kind of outsized purchases of oil as the recent Treasury spree of corporate assets of $1 trillion. A far smaller investment during the pandemic-caused crash of oil prices in April 2020 could have been easily stopped oil from slipping into the "silly zone" of the teens and even ridiculously into negative territory. Indeed, much of the asset buying of the Fed during the Spring of 2020 were distressed oil assets from producers reeling from collapsing oil prices. It would have been far more efficacious, and a heck of a lot cheaper, if the Treasury Department devoted some of its money into oil instead of these CCC- and even lower-rated bonds. There are good, practical reasons to devote some of that cash to the commodity itself as opposed to the bonds of distressed oil companies: One thing we know for sure is that oil will be worth something again in the future. But that can hardly be said for many of the distressed assets (many of them oil assets) that the Federal Reserve put on its books during the COVID-19 crisis. Many of those will prove to be worth less than the paper they're printed on.

Obviously, such a systemic program of buying and selling of oil by the United States needs to be under strict oversight, so that it is neither used as a proxy "bailout" for oil companies during tough times, nor as a politically motivated proxy "tax rebate" for consumers, delivered during election years when prices spike. A simple mathematical formula that measures the percentage change of prices over time can simply steady prices both if they suddenly crash, as well as if they unexpectedly and rapidly spike.

This seems an important improvement on the current use of the Strategic Petroleum Reserve, benefiting both oil companies in bad times and consumers in good times—and all of us in steadier oil markets.

A FINAL WORD ON MARKETS

Market analysis is difficult and subject to interpretation. And much of what I'm suggesting necessarily puts upwards pressure on oil prices. That's what we need, I think, to supercharge motion towards natural gas and renewables.

But almost all economists I read will tell you that rising oil prices are especially destructive to the economy at large, and they might discard the entire premise of this book based on that view alone.

I am not an economist. But I have witnessed markets on a daily basis since I first walked into the oil pits in 1982. During that time, I have focused particularly on how other stock, bond, and commodity markets, and the economy at large can affect oil prices. I've also charted the opposite effects: how changing oil prices can impact the U.S. economy as a whole. And I'll tell you, I don't buy it. I have not seen the outsized effects on the economy or consumers at large (good or bad) from either a low or a high oil price. Do I have a load of lovely-looking charts and studies to prove this to you, the kind of inundation that truly expert economists can produce? I certainly don't. But I have traded oil during some of the most robust periods of global growth and U.S. growth, and during some of the worst, and I've not noticed any consistent correlation.

Figure 11.6 shows the change in annual GDP percentage growth from 1990 to 2018. In general, throughout these 30 years, we've seen pretty steady growth, punctuated by negative growth (recessions) mostly triggered by other economic collapses (the tech bubble in 2000 and the credit crisis of 2008 being the two most glaring).

Did oil prices matter to either the good times or the bad times? If they did, it wasn't much of an effect, that's for sure.

Figure 11.6.
Percent Change in U.S. Gross Domestic Product (GDP) (1990 - 2018)

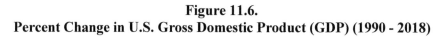
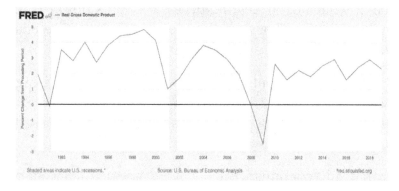

It seems to me that oil (and energy in general) is one of those very INELASTIC inputs, to use an economics word. In plain speak, we can say that whether we are experiencing good times or bad, the need for energy—that is, for oil, natural gas, electricity, whatever—stays pretty much the same, and folks seem to find the money to get what they need when they need it and make those adjustments, without sacrificing much else. As I've said often in this book, oil demand seems to increase by 1 million barrels a day a year, whether prices are high or low. The only time demand craters is when the global economy does—and that's not really attributable to oil prices, is it? Even during the crash of 2008, oil prices had been dropping like a rock, having seen their height in July, when the fall of Lehman Brothers and the real start of the financial crisis began in October.

In any event, I think I'll end this book by saying that not much will be hurt by helping oil prices to follow their natural progression higher, as every other asset has.

And a whole lot could be helped. It might even save the world.

A Last Word

I was more than a year into the writing of this book when the coronavirus swept through. And it changed everything.

My book was intended to address a different set of market circumstances than the ones I've been looking at since March 2020, and the ones likely to remain for the next few years, as far as I can tell. The economic fallout from the coronavirus looks to me to be very long-lasting: there is the obvious dramatic decline in global growth; businesses are going bankrupt in every sector under the sun; unemployment is racing higher; whole sectors of the economy are going to need a bailout and saddle the federal government with debts no one can guess how large. Nothing but a vaccine (which looks at best to perhaps arrive in the spring of 2021) will deliver the confidence to consumers to take up again the spending that has been the staple of U.S. economic success—which still 70% of our economy relies on. Until that vaccine, I don't see anything but disaster for restaurants, theaters, retail shops, travel, sports and recreation, hotels – the list is endless.

In energy, the picture is bleaker, if that's possible. Gasoline consumption, in the first few months of the COVID-19 outbreak, was down nearly 50%. That kind of drop in energy use has ripple effects that are wide, and from my perch today, it's too soon to see how manageable (or unmanageable) they'll be. But think about it: if no one is going much of anywhere for a year or more out of fear of infection, you don't need your car much anymore. If you were working and laid off, you really can't afford one anyway.

Now you've got a whole lot of people who are looking to sell their cars, or even, if they have one of the 30 million leases in this country, looking to give those cars back to the banks that financed them. Car prices, like oil prices, will plummet. Defaulting loans on cars that are now worth far less puts banks at risk, and we know from 2008 what it takes to make that right. In addition, auto makers suddenly can't sell new cars, with all the cheap used ones out there. Auto parts and auto repair shops see their activity drop massively...You can see where this is heading.

Widespread deflation—which is what I'm talking about—is the worst 4-letter word in economics. It was the overwhelming characteristic of the Great Depression and was the main reason that it lasted so long, compared to other economic downturns. Of course, deficit spending, FDR's New Deal, and industrialization to gear up for WWII finally turned around the Depression. But with interest rates at zero, a U.S. military that is already bloated, and a U.S. President who seems solely interested in keeping the stock market up, but otherwise couldn't resemble FDR any less, it's unlikely any of that old playbook will work this time around.

So where does that leave Energy?

My book's thesis was simple: to get to a renewable future, we most needed to see renewables competitive with global oil and natural gas. And the simplest way to do that was to find a path to make either renewables a lot cheaper or fossil fuels a lot more expensive.

I still see (despite the coronavirus) the path to more expensive fossil fuels a lot easier (and more beneficial to the planet and everyone's bottom line) than the current slow grind and fast-approaching limits of technology making renewables significantly cheaper. Technology and its advancements are amazing, incredible, and mind-boggling, but they come when they're able, not always where they're hoped. For example, and despite great strides in cheaper manufacturing techniques, the base mechanism of how solar panels make electricity hasn't changed or improved its efficiency much since the 1960s.

I saw many hurdles to what I think is the "natural" progression of energy prices going higher: the structure of energy markets, the mismanagement of shale oil, the lack of a coherent policy in Washington, the myth of energy independence as a worthwhile goal to continue to pursue. But I saw reasonable responses to all of these, all of which I laid out in this book. I think most of these suggestions would deliver enormous benefits across the board—for energy companies, for investors, for plain working people, and, of course, for our environment.

What coronavirus has done, however, is move the timeline that I saw further back—at least a year, but possibly even three or four years. Quite simply, the gluts of oil and gas that will land on the markets from the deflationary recession I see coming, and the time it will take for those surpluses to clear, will keep oil and gas prices low for a very long time to come, perhaps even if every suggestion of mine is put into action. Low fossil fuel prices will continue to inspire the world to use fossil fuels when they need energy, and not to invest in renewables instead. The transition will be even slower now than before. And the transition was far, far too slow before.

It's not all bad news. The massive and immediate slowdown of fossil fuel use caused by the coronavirus has given the Earth a well-deserved break from the daily onslaught of carbon. There are constant reports of major cities with cleaner air than they've seen in 50 years, and wild animals venturing into empty, locked-down city streets to reclaim territories they were forced from more than a century ago. I've even heard that the Earth is actually vibrating less, with the slowdown of human motion caused by nationwide lock-downs.

But when all "gets back to normal," whenever (or whatever) that is, we'll still have a global oil and gas market that will be under severe price pressure, and more time will be lost getting to the kind of sustainable future we all need to see.

I started writing this book in haste, feeling a need to get this out there as soon as possible, with dire global warning predictions blanketing the news media. However, I now feel like this book will arrive with the time to think about and digest its ideas—and perhaps to craft some critically important, environmentally sound strategies for the future.

As oil and natural gas gluts clear and prices resume their upwards trajectory (which they inevitably must), maybe some of the mistakes we've made in Washington and on Wall Street that I saw when writing this book won't be repeated, and we'll find a way to be smarter about oil and gas, solar, and wind power. And maybe we'll see a smarter way to get there from here.

One can only hope.

Index

oil contracts, 122, 149-153, 160

oil demand, 22-23, Figure 1.4, 32-35, 47-48, Figure 3.2, 52, 129, 132, 134, 137-142, Figure 7.1, 146, 149, 152, 188, 205-207, 223, 225, 231

oil drilling, 11-12, 31-32, 40, Figure 3.4, 50-51, 56-67, 114-115, 118-127, Figure 9.2, 170-172, 177

oil futures, 1, 31, 86, 137, 139, 149, 150-158, 208, 223

oil grading, 31-32, 53-60, Figure 3.5, 186-188

oil prices, 10-12, Figure 1.1, 15-19, 23, 25-37, 43-47, Figure 3.1, 49, 52, 55, 57, 64, 66-67, 69-79, Figure 4.1, 85-87, 94, 10-106, 114-115, 118-119, 121-124, 127-129, 132, 134-147, 148-154, 157-159, 161-178, Figure 9.1, 184-184, Figure 10.2, 188-189, 191, 197, 206-209, 212-217, 221, 223-231, Figure 11.5, 234-235

Oil's Endless Bid, 84, 151, 223, 225

OPEC, 1, 12-13, 34, 48, 58, 60, 65-67, Figure 4.1, 70-71, 73, 76-80, 134, 138, 144-145, 149, 152, 159, 161, 163-172, 174-175, 178, 221

Orinoco, 55-56

Papa, Mark, 108-110

Paris Climate Accords, 3, 22, 92, 94, 204, 207, 221

Payroll Protection Plan, 155

peak oil theory, 30-31

Permian Basin, 61-62, 108,112, 115, 126, 138, 193, Figure 10.4, 197, 209

Peters, Enno, 116, Figure 6.2

CPSIA information can be obtained
at www.ICGtesting.com
Printed in the USA
LVHW081806310822
727309LV00004B/653

9 780996 489768